Preaching Holiness Effectively

PREACHING
HOLINESS
EFFECTIVELY

by

Mel-Thomas Rothwell

BEACON HILL PRESS OF KANSAS CITY
Kansas City, Missouri

Permission to quote from the following copyrighted versions is acknowledged with appreciation:

The Holy Bible, New International Version (NIV), copyright © 1978 by the New York International Bible Society.

New American Standard Bible (NASB), © The Lockman Foundation, 1960, 1962, 1968, 1971, 1972, 1973, 1975, 1977.

The *New English Bible* (NEB), © The Delegates of the Oxford University Press and The Syndics of the Cambridge University Press, 1961, 1970.

The *Revised Standard Version of the Bible* (RSV), copyrighted 1946, 1952, © 1971, 1973.

Good News Bible, Today's English Version (TEV)—Old Testament © American Bible Society, 1976; New Testament © American Bible Society, 1966, 1971, 1976.

To Helen, my wife

Contents

Foreword

It is a personal joy to me to introduce *Preaching Holiness Effectively* from the pen of Dr. Mel-Thomas Rothwell, whose life and ministry have been close to me for more than 40 years.

The book itself flows from the mind and heart and life of the author. He has been very well known as a revivalist and camp meeting evangelist, and as a reliable scholar through all these years.

His style reflects his early years in newspaper reporting. He has a way with words. Also, his scholarship affords him an excellent theological vocabulary and understanding, but he does not get bogged down in "pedantic trivia."

I can readily foresee that this book will find a permanent place in our college and Bible college classrooms at home and abroad. It is full of practical guidance and helpfulness for pastors as well as evangelists. It should help all of us in our teaching ministry both with respect to content of message and style of presentation.

Above all, Dr. Mel-Thomas (as I call him) is readable. The drive of his message is that "we must preach holiness amiably"—for it is winsome and right.

"These are words you may trust" (Titus 3:8, NEB).

This book belongs in every pastor's library and study desk.

—SAMUEL YOUNG
General Superintendent Emeritus

Preface

Preaching Holiness Effectively does not come to the reader as the finished work of a master in preaching.

Rather, it issues compassionately from the heart and mind of one long committed to the conviction that holiness can, and must, be proclaimed effectively.

Why use the term *effective?*

Effective is rich with latent meaning. It is used generally when one plans to achieve a desired result. In addition, among its many cognates are words of moving inference and force which grant the pulpit speaker related depths and wider latitudes.

The term *effective* is used here chiefly to accentuate the biblical truth that the preaching of holiness is not an experiment, with the overshadowing risk, or peril, of a dry run; nor is it an option, a preference rationally worked out in a professional dialogue on opposing theological points of view.

As summarily stated in *God, Man, and Salvation,* the highly regarded recent biblical theology written by three theologians of the Church of the Nazarene, "The never-ending task of the Church is to interpret its faith to the contemporary world. To do this requires an understanding of what is essential to the faith and what is incidental. Failure at this point not only cripples personal piety; it garbles the proclamation of the gospel to the world."[1] Hence, the viable essentials in understanding and proclamation in the preaching of holiness largely constitute the discourse herein incorporated.

To preach holiness effectively proposes and assures

the proclamation of the biblical tenets of the fundamental teaching in such a way and in such a spirit that the believer, on hearing the call, will be enlightened and potently encouraged to seek entire sanctification as a distinct, second-crisis experience, after the new birth.

Holiness is the unique, scripturally endorsed relation between God and His redeemed people; access to the beautiful grace can be clearly elucidated so as to make certain the believer's triumphant entrance.

Thus, it is not a matter of discretion, subject to the beck and call of human desire or the sway of reason, but it is the indispensable condition on which we will see God. Providently God's Word cautions, "Make every effort to live in peace with all men and to be holy; without holiness no one will see the Lord" (Heb. 12:14, NIV).

Acknowledgments

Primarily, a loving, devoted wife has been my mainstay and source of encouragement throughout the entire undertaking. Helen has read the manuscript three times, corrected it for grammar and all errors, and she has provided invaluable suggestions regarding form, design, and readability.

Prof. Lawrence Snell, professor emeritus of Bethany Nazarene College, typed the entire manuscript. He proved himself an able, sincere friend; he has helped make the writing a delight, always on time, always revealing an attitude of genuine Christian concern.

Finally, I have scanned the horizons of knowledge and faith from the shoulders of others who have preceded me, profiting by their success, and to them I am forever obligated.

Introduction

A new book is conventionally welcomed by discriminating reading circles in direct relation to the particular benefit those readers hope to derive from its contribution.

To capture the attention of the reader, therefore, any publication must touch vitally that individual's interest as a creative person. Its subject matter must deal essentially and viably with whatever the scanning or scrutinizing reader has in mind and purpose. If we can regard the writer-reader encounter as candid, curious minds at work, with understanding as the aim, a better mutual rule and relation can be established.

Preaching Holiness Effectively is directed primarily to the twofold relation involved in proclaiming holiness: the individual makeup of the preacher and the peerless content of the message. The preacher as a person is called upon to proclaim God's crowning truth to the other members of his race. This unparalleled mission is divinely approved and implemented by God's own unctious, enabling presence. God and human person in active sharing cojointly carry out the unique responsibility of declaring the Living, Redeeming Word.

Hence, the primacies of the book are clear-cut: First, What is God's place and work as Surety for the Holy; and second, What is man's part as the human copartner in the grand plan of redemption? The Bible, when properly understood as an anchor of divine truth, and man, God's fellow worker as a contemporary mortal being, underscore the entire endeavor of the research, with God's purpose and method as revealed in the Word of God carefully related to finite diversity and imperfections.

Every committed person in God's fellowship is a potential minister; none are excluded on account of racial, social, national, or individual differences. Bible preaching is a declaration of the whole gospel by the whole person, an exercise of the full range of the preacher's being and acumen. For a case in point, one might refer to Christ's apostolate, where widely differentiated human traits and aptitudes were fashioned into a functional mastery and service. Conflicting distinctions as prolific as only the endowed human personality incorporates them confronted the Master, who welded divergent features into a world-shaking striking force of unity and goodwill.

Evidently God has no problem with differences in dedicated people; on the contrary, they mark His path through history. Diversity and spontaneity have been the preacher's hallmark from New Testament times. But what of the Old Testament line of prophets? Could one find a more dissimilar roster of individuals? Be gone the fear of change! We should welcome its ruddy freshness and unspoiled cutting edge. Whereas there is no merit in change for change's sake—historical Hericletian flux (change is king)—neither is there security where progress has come to a standstill.

Light is shed on leading holiness terms as a definitive help to a more critical understanding of the whole thesis. Terminology, however, does not become a battlefield darkly littered with the relics of war. The crucial use of such terms as *crisis, process, growth, change, progress,* and *entire* in *entire sanctification* highlights the involved areas of this study so that emphasis falls on pertinent issues and thought. Traditional positions and opinions are communicated in the authentic contemporary posture, in a painstaking and honest respect for both. No spasmodic grievance of personal or denominational consequence deflects or turns the tide of

Bible truth in its onward redemptive thrust, with holiness as its standard.

This book puts the pulpit and pew together in a living-crisis experience. Guarded attention is given to the propriety and simple dignity of the pulpit. Ideas are worked out to assure its most compelling and persuasive advantage and utility. Hence, the preacher should find stimulating and refreshing precepts and guidelines which should lay open wide latitudes of useful resources. The place and use of method, or technique, in the breakdown of parts and chapters hopefully assure easy accessibility.

The pew is prophetically and responsibly linked to the pulpit, a relationship undeniably social and political, and yet primarily personal. Personal salvation, the heart of Christianity, embraces a far broader concern in the spiritual, social, and even political welfare of all members of any congregation than is generally granted. It is in that glow-or-glare malaise that holiness must be declared with no uncertain sound. That is the living-crisis experience for the pulpit servant and his listening audience. In brief, this work is thoughtfully and practically geared to the total function of the preacher in the pulpit proficiency of proclaiming Bible holiness to eternity-bound men and women who honor him by making an effort to hear and learn.

Based on the writer's contacts and experiences, a timely need has already opened for the type of awareness and remedial information explored and stressed within these pages.

Holiness is alive and doing well! Let us praise God for its enduring grace and preach it with confidence and joy!

The book is divided into two parts: Part I deals with the *certification* of holiness in the Word of God. Thus, holiness is validated. Further division of the part shows how its purpose and force are released through the strategic functions and responsibilities of the pulpit and church. First, a firm biblical foundation is laid to support the favor and benefaction of holiness, which alone can yoke God and man in righteous fellowship. On this basis the thesis treats avidly the place of doctrine, evangelism, and pastoral service in the proclamation structure, disciplines which largely constitute the work of the Holy Spirit in implementing and extending the kingdom of God in the church and in the world.

With the foundation for certification resting solidly and durably on the Living Word, the theme moves on to the second crucial relationship, that of the preacher. Part II enlarges and develops the holiness cause by giving consideration to the preacher as a person and as a prophet. The writer is not aware of other volumes in print which treat the personal traits of the preacher in the same down-to-earth style, with true deference for individuality and freedom in the pulpit. Indispensable freedom, nonetheless, does not give occasion for the preacher to cop out in critical issues, as the remainder of the part notes in detail.

The strength of *affirmation*, the positive in contradistinction to negation, is brought into penetrating light; holiness as *attractive*, in contrast to the ugly and repulsive tags too often attached to it, makes it a "thing of beauty, and a joy forever"; a scriptural and understandable resolution of *fire* finds a weighty and imperative place in a chapter on being *ardent*; and finally and suitably the whole thesis is wrapped up in perfect love and wholeness in a chapter urging *amiability*, which commits the entire endeavor to the beauty and transport of divine love. In Part II, *validation* of the Word of God is combined and harmonized with *variation* in the servant, the bearer of that Word.

Hence, a unique interrelation between God and His ministering servant particularizes the preacher in conscious rapport, an association kept alive by a dynamic, renewing fellowship and intelligent interchange. *Unique* from its French origin, means the only one of its kind, not some-

16

thing rare or outstanding by a scaling of degrees. Thus, God's messenger is marked by a "unique" anointing and confirmation of the Holy Spirit, a distinct divine unction for which there is neither effective human invention nor replacement.

This piece of writing is programmed and projected to bring the Bible concept of uniqueness to clear and applicable understanding in reference to preaching holiness. No stand-in or prime-time surrogate can take its place. The thesis tries to show emphatically that human diversity is complemented and enhanced by the divine anointing, not toned down or revoked by the extraordinary "only" which obtains between God and finite man. Timothy L. Smith puts it well, "The promise of the continual sanctifying presence of the Holy Spirit in the Body of Christ is as trustworthy now as it was at Pentecost."[1] The author places priority on the Bible and its central truth, and on the watchman and his message, which should reflect, it is believed God's charge to Ezekiel: "Mortal man, I am making you a watchman for the nation of Israel" (3:17, TEV).

The reader must keep in mind that this volume does not propose to explore all the exegetical and hermeneutical landmarks of theology. Rather, we again stress that it attempts to put together the place and relation of God and the preacher in the course of full redemption, a soundly biblical approach prompting a prayerful search for the ideal.

Consequently, the purpose and presentation herein pursued makes heavy documentation dispensable and, perhaps, inadvisable. References to other sources obtain only when some vantage point is needed for light and elevation in the reading experience. Documentation inclines the movement to analysis and depth study largely, whereas a guarded use of it tends to keep the action going and the perspective clear. This view in no wise means to cast aspersions on high-quality research in which exegesis and critical interpretation are the mainstays. The aim of this book is to encourage fairly rapid transit without sacrificing representative depth.

A half century of holiness preaching, an academically programmed education, and, primarily and preciously, compassionate prayer prompt the author to offer *Preaching Holiness Effectively* as the outreach of a loving hand to scores of young preachers of many denominations who have inquired of him, "How shall we preach holiness?"

Part I

CERTIFICATION (Validation)

1

Preaching Holiness

BIBLICALLY

And a highway will be there, a roadway,
And it will be called the Highway of Holiness.
The unclean will not travel on it,
But it will be for him who walks that way,
And fools will not wander on it.
Isa. 35:8, NASB

Holiness as the lifeline of reality begins in Genesis and moves perceptibly and invariably through every book of the Old and New Testaments to its crowning moment in the final Revelation.

Although the evidence is seemingly fragmentary and isolated at times, in the grand scale the perspective of holiness in eternal redemption falls gracefully and eloquently into place. This overview is observed when the extraordinary scope of its diversity and inference is submitted to the discernments of faith and the grasp of reason where true wisdom comes to light. "The true wisdom, Paul says, is not to be found in Greek philosophy, but only in Christ: and that not speculatively but experientially . . . (1 Cor. 1:30, NIV)."[1]

A. The Bible: God's Handbook on Holiness

The Bible is God's handbook on holiness, a manual on its motivation, its mobility, and its morality. In it is the record and fulfillment of the inception, providence, and final elevation of holiness in His millennia-spanning plan of redemption. All other issues which arise in the ongoing stream of salvation must inevitably somehow relate to holiness, if they in any real sense relate to God. Every expression of His being, every intricate line of His existence, leads to or from holiness, including the written revelation.

Every angle and design of Bible history and Christian culture is the expression of holiness in some redemptive form. Whether a contextual detail or a transcending dispensational truth, it matters not; holiness at each interrelating moment and point is the clue to valid and realistic Christian insight.

From "In the beginning God" (Gen. 1:1) to "Even so, come, Lord Jesus" (Rev. 22:20), the way of holiness is reaffirmed and distinctly placed on record. It is expressed or inferred in many terms, their synonyms, or other cognate expressions, which in some way and for some decisive reason pertain to the essential meaning of holiness: reflecting it, bearing on it, or belonging to it.

If the magnitude and magnificence of the Word of God were reduced to a single word, or one idea, it would be *holiness*.[2] Holiness is the being and activity of God; it has no rival or real contenders. The Holy is one in idea and reality. Its course of action is manifested by a holy conduct and practice. "And a highway will be there; it will be called the Way of Holiness" (Isa. 35:8, NIV).

B. Unity in Testamental Scope and Meaning

"The emphasis of the Old Testament is upon the holiness of God."[3] We also note that the emphasis of the New

Testament is upon the love of God, which eventuated in the expression "the God of holy love," used first by Peter Forsyth and later by William Temple and H. Orton Wiley.[4]

Holiness in the Old Testament inheres largely in man's relationship to God through ordinance, ceremony, and command. Things and times were regarded holy by the worthiness acquired in their relation to God. Both the Old and New Testaments set forth positional holiness at this point, but the "New Testament does not permit a sanctity which remains positional only. 'Become what you are' is the demand. Saints must be saintly. Believers are 'called to be saints' (Rom. 1:7; 1 Cor. 1:21)—not by appellation only, but by vocation."[5]

Thus, man is never regarded holy while he is in any attitude or position of disobedience, or while he is engaged in idolatry. Sin is the principal unity-breaker in God's relationship to man. As Donald S. Metz has put it forthrightly, "The ultimate spiritual antithesis is the opposition between holiness and sin. Man was designed for holiness, created in holiness, and destined for holiness."[6] Then, sin alone can effect the deadly partition between God and man, rending that harmony which would otherwise mark their holy union (Isa. 59:2).

The Old Testament and rabbinic literature point to God as "the Holy One." Gustaf Aulén maintains that "holiness is the foundation on which the whole conception of God rests. Every statement about God, whether in reference to His love, power, righteousness . . . ceases to be affirmation about God when it is not projected against the background of His holiness."[7]

John Wick Bowman subsumes holiness under two orders, the priestly and the prophetic. In the priestly order, holiness, persons, and things were set apart, dedicated by ceremony; whereas in prophetic holiness, which had a prominent ethical content, only persons could be sanctified. Bowman asserts that "the New Testament, finally, takes up only the prophetic side of the term and perpetuates it. All Christians are to be 'saints' (holy ones—Rom. 1: 7), that is, ethically holy, separated, consecrated to God's service (Mark 6:20; John 17:17), that they may have fellowship with a holy God (Acts 9:13; Rom. 1:7; Heb. 6:10; Rev. 5:8)."[8]

A highly regarded source affirms that "Personal piety in the Old Testament is frequently described in terms of holiness. Israel had early been called to be a 'holy nation' (Exod. 19:6; Lev. 19:2; 20:26)."[9]

The ascription of holiness involved both cultic or ritual and moral or ethical holiness. The negative-positive equation held here, for it was not merely separation from something—other nations—that made Israel holy, but in addition it was Israel's further relation to God. The void of the negative cannot sanctify; it may separate. In a positive sequence the love union with God completes, or makes perfect, the sanctifying process. We are not only saved from something, we are blessedly saved to something: to Someone.

C. Sound Biblical Theology Needed

To avoid erosion on one hand, or clutter and accumulation on the other, the teaching and preaching of holiness needs to be grounded in sound biblical theology. The more guarded the term "holy" is used in its primary meaning in the Bible, the clearer its understanding, vitality, and value in the church, and especially in the believer, become. Whereas biblical theology is not a terminal study, it is the only adequate way to secure a safe exegetical foundation for systematic theology. Olin A. Curtis has put it lucidly, "The whole Bible must be philosophically grasped as a Christian unity which is manifested in variety."[10]

The purpose of scholarly biblical theology is not to become a theology within a theology. Nor is it a foster parent or patron in the course of systematic theology; it is rather fully and inextricably absorbed into its scope and utility. Biblical theology tries to elicit reliably the exact meaning as it came from the prophet's lips or from historical events. If there is any hazard, it is in the possibility of a "learned aloofness" which might cause a partition in the theological ranks.

In direct relation to biblical theology a unitary system of theological thinking needs expression and finds it in systematic theology, in which the doctrines of the church are ordered by a relational methodology of scriptural teachings and meanings. It is the systematic pertinence that is important if doctrine is to be the basis of teaching and also have historical significance. Perhaps we should note that this is not what Barth and Brunner meant by *dogmatics*, which is defined by Tillich as "the statement of the doctrinal tradition for our present situation."[11] Dogmatics must be set in the contemporary and the dogmatician must not be a system builder, for, said Brunner, reflecting Barth's view also, "Rigid unity of thought, in dogmatics, is the infallible sign of error . . . Dogmatics as a system, even when it intends to be a system of revelation, is the misguided dominion of the rational element over faith."[12]

Also subtle and dangerous is a threat from the opposite pole. In an article "Holiness Evangelism in the 80s," Paul R. Orjala warned of that innocentlike hazard: "In the process, we must help our people clearly understand the Bible doctrine of holiness. There is a lot of unbiblical 'folk theology' on holiness that is inadequate and even harmful. We need to take care about how we make our own statements about holiness, to be sure that we are biblical and that we do not make careless statements that lead people to expect less or more than what the Bible teaches about the sanctified life."[13]

How timely Dr. Orjala's entreaty, and how better

could we obey it than to secure our Bible grounds on holiness through the service of biblical theology. For a clear, explicit definition of biblical theology may we return to *God, Man, and Salvation,* where it is said to be "the application of principles of logical thought, both inductive and deductive, to the statements, facts, data, and events of the Scriptures considered in their historical context with a view to developing comprehensive patterns of interpretation."[14] The high purpose and value of biblical theology is to isolate from Bible truth the folklore which attaches to traditional religion as history moves forward.

Community folktales and legends built up over the years tend to become a part of common religious practice and may even replace original Bible teaching. "What Uncle Ebe believed" or "the way we've always done it" may have sentimental value, but if carried far enough it can become a clear case of folk theology. The theologians need not draw back into their academic shells, nor should the traditionalists rush back to the brush arbors. We are one in calling and purpose. May God keep our hearts warm, our minds clear, and our hands busy; the greatest hour in history has struck, as Dr. Chapman proclaimed—it is "All Out for Souls!"

D. Principles and Priorities

Wounded and torn apart by sin in the original state, the beautiful and holy relationship between God and His image-bearing creature, man, had to be restored by atonement. A long-range comprehensive plan of redemption went into effect immediately. The oneness of Eden, rent by the culpable act of sin, was reinstituted by the sacrifice of His own Son on Calvary, "that they may be one, just as We are one" (John 17:22, NASB).

Oneness in this delicate, yet inseverable bond is forthrightly based on a sanctifying act and walk—an act by which the sin-prone is made love-allied, and the ensuing walk credits and honors the transformed union. The magnificent transaction, a sinner made whole, eventuates in the walk alluded to in the Scriptures by the description, "The one who says he abides in Him ought himself to walk in the same manner as He walked" (1 John 2:6, NASB). Christ in you is dynamic life, not pied-piper idealism associated with some theological choice. Rather, "By this is My Father glorified, that you bear much fruit, and so prove to be My disciples" (John 15:8, NASB).

1. The Trilogy of Redemption: Obedience, Love, and Cleansing

Three basic principles, although each in its own sense is complete, are closely related and develop a single theme, the Trilogy of Redemption. Careful analysis of these primary principles as comprehensive and fundamental laws and doctrines will reveal in the end why God chose them. All spiritual, moral, social, or even political ramifications found in the Word of God in some primary sense relate to these axiomatic guidelines.

The underlying groundwork in the extraordinary plan of redemption is precisely the same for both Testaments: obedience, love, and cleansing. As has been indicated, all salvation effort and means vitally engage these basic principles. For instance, man's approach to God is not universally uniform; but if he is in the Kingdom, regardless of custom or detail of worship, his holy walk will bear the hallmark of obedience, love, and cleansing from sin. If these sacred landmarks are missing in his theology and life, so is the Savior, Jesus Christ.

a. Obedience

Obedience is the minimal essential of relationship between God and man. Obey and live, God commanded, but in wisdom and justice, with infinite foresight, He made provision for the reclamation of those who by disobedience fell. Obedience became the standard of the righteous relation in man's recovery. Remember God's instructions to Abraham: "Walk before me, and be thou perfect" (Gen. 17:1). Of Moses, who built an altar at the foot of the mountain, we read, "Then he took the book of the covenant and read it in the hearing of the people; and they said, 'All that the Lord has spoken we will do, and we will be obedient!'" (Exod. 24:7, NASB). On the contrary, disobedience pays off in lethal coin; Israel hears God's voice as she is poised to cross Jordan, "Like the nations that the Lord makes to perish before you, so you shall perish; because you would not listen to the voice of the Lord your God" (Deut. 8:20, NASB).

In the Old Testament obedience always alludes to a law, statute, ordinance, or ceremony. Note, for instance, Gen. 17: 1; Exod. 22:31; Lev. 19:2; and Ezek. 11:20. The Lord, speaking through Ezekiel, stipulates, "Walk in my statutes, and keep mine ordinances, and do them" (11:20).

The New Testament enjoins obedience as the certification of love, seen transparently in Christ's conditional citation to the disciples, "If you love Me, you will keep My commandments" (John 14:15, NASB). In his First Epistle, John adds appending instruction when he says, "Little children, let us not love with word or with tongue, but in deed and truth" (3:18, NASB). Holiness cannot be compatible with moral otherness; human frailty and shortcomings, yes, but never with willful moral mutiny. The offender is cast out, not merely his unrighteous behavior; if he does not obey, he does not belong. The theological attempt to "doctor" his fellowship only is akin to rubbing salve on the bruises of a dead man. Indeed, the idea of a sinning religion is as foreign to one Testament as it is to the other.

Throughout the Word of God man is called to obedience, and God has made ample provision to fulfill His demand. At no time does the requirement exceed human capability or the provisions of grace. Man answers to moral integrity, not to finite infirmity. No frailty or vulnerability of creaturehood rules out a full surrender of his will to God's known purpose. So long as man consents willingly to God's authority, all of his failures and imperfections are covered by the Atonement.

It would be unwise to give an issue unwarranted emphasis, but who in the light of history dare disclaim the virtue and value of discipline and self-control? Obedience promotes self-mastery and thus insures discipline. As Goethe put it, "In der Beschrankrung zeigt sich erst der Meister" (It is in self-limitation that a master first shows himself).[15] Paul reminds the Corinthians in his first letter, "Everyone who competes in the games goes into strict training" (9:25, NIV). At the core of discipline and success is obedience, with perfection as its goal. Whether or not perfection will be reached, or can be reached, is beside the question at this point. Without perfection as target the cord of endeavor is tragically severed, and life lapses into aimless bewilderment.

One is reminded of Nietzsche's abject, forlorn wail in his depressed solitude, speaking of nihilism: "This weirdest of all guests . . . stands before the door."[16] Mocking the "frightening implications" of space, Pascal lends great force by his eloquence: "Cast into the infinite immensity of spaces of which I am ignorant, and which know me not, I am frightened."[17] Jonas' charge that Pascal's God is *agnostos theos*, an unknown god, is evidently the nihilist's problem, not the Christian's. Nor Pascal's, for that matter; recall his assertion that the heart has "reason" that reason knows nothing about.

b. Love

The authentic and active ground of obedience and law-keeping in the plan of salvation is love, the love of God.

Love is equally contained in both Testaments, although

its role and province may vary. Law marks the devotion of the obedient in the Old Testament, whereas the latitude of love becomes the New Testament norm. Love underlies both Testaments with total consecration and commitment as the heartbeat of integrity.

The concept of love, especially perfect love, is not peculiar to the New Testament, as many may suppose; but it is basic to God's relationship with man, their oneness, fellowship, and working agreement. As early as Deuteronomy the eminence of love gets attention: "And thou shalt love the Lord thy God with all thine heart, and with all thy soul, and with all thy might" (6:5). Jesus himself set down the New Testament equivalent (Mark 12:30).

How a finite creature fits into a plan involving perfection provokes no end of discordant debate. A perfection embracing the natural attributes of God in infinite measure need not even be argued. Human beings may imitate the divine attributes, but in no way can they approximate them. The hunt is over before the chase begins; being God is not an achievement open to man. Neither by creation nor by dictum does God expect absolute perfection from man. He has wisely allotted responsibility only within the range of capability. However, a kind of perfection for man in unmistakable diction is incorporated in the Sermon on the Mount: "Therefore you are to be perfect, as your heavenly Father is perfect" (Matt. 5:48, NASB).

There is no escape from the divine plan that man is to be perfect. And there can be scarcely any doubt in what sense perfection applies when the context is read. It is love. If God's child cannot love Him with all his heart, soul, mind, and strength, then the divine expectation is too high. Anything less than perfect love commits man to a sliding scale of values, with scant light as to the probable outcome. The case for the positive is lost, and skepticism raps loudly at the door.

The idea of perfection in man faces a hostile paradox, as any trained theologian, or even an untutored believer, would not deny. All one has to do is reflect on it, or try to live it or live with it, and the integrity of perfection comes up for review. Yet, no less authority than the Word of God, without ambiguity or mincing of terms, proposes perfection as a standard. Too often some theologians respond as though it were a predicament for logic to handle. Rationalize if we will, but better to obey. As Metz observes, "Logically it appears to be a contradiction. Experientially, it is reality."[18] "A Christian may live in a spiritual and ethical state of holiness," he continues. "The essence of this state of holiness, or perfection, is love to God and man, purity of motivation, and cleansing from inherent sin. But because of finite qualities which bear the scars of sin, this same believer will not perfectly fulfill God's law. Thus, 'perfection in one respect, and imperfection in another, may consistently meet in the same person; as he may be perfect in one sense, while imperfect in another.'"

Wisely, the Bible holds perfection in responsible balance, requiring ability and maturity on the creature's part. On that account, the only perfection within reach of the finite being is an excellence adaptable to his existence: all-out commitment to God's will, a crisis; and then an all-pervading walk with God, a process. A further, final stipulation: Perfection here does not imply absolute competence; rather, it submits the idea of completion, an undertaking wherein man experiences and lives the power of full salvation. He is not perfect like God, he is perfect as God is perfect in love.

Immeasurably small infractions are sin as anything is sin that varies from the infallible canon. How then can man be perfect? His will has not changed, he still loves God with all his heart, soul, mind, and strength, and loves his neighbor as himself. What, then, has changed? Wherein did he sin? He sinned in the absolute sense because his performance fell far short of God's infallible canon and conduct. For the creature there is a vast difference between being willing and having the skill to perform.

For that reason, the Father's child loving Him perfectly may be guilty of a flaw of human consequence, chargeable to his finite frame but not to his moral willingness. How frequently we have heard a child, moving to his own defense, declare stoutly, "I didn't mean to do it." We are going to have to honor that qualified defense or scrap a lot of theology. A theology that cannot account for the evident difference between an involuntary and voluntary act is definitely expendable by the Bible standard.

We are inquirers after a better way! We need not fear the impact and import of God's holy Word if we walk in the light of the Scriptures as God has plainly revealed it to us, distinctly and unmistakably in Matt. 5:48; Mark 12:30-31; and 1 Pet. 1:16.

With abundant headwaters in the Old Testament, the mighty stream of salvation pours its refreshing waters of love and peace into the channels of the New Testament, completing and realizing its purpose and plan. Arising in command but completed in Christ, love keeps redemption on course from the Garden to the Cross. John faultlessly inscribes it in his first letter:

> In this is love, not that we loved God, but that He loved us and sent His Son to be the propitiation for our sins. Beloved, if God so loved us, we also ought to love one another (4:10-11, NASB).

c. Cleansing (or Purification)

"Cleansing" heads a category of terms which indicate how God proposes to deal with sin. He can strike no bargain with sin; holiness and sin are forever incompatible. Sin must go and the mode is destruction. The term "destruction" has several meanings in the Scriptures. In reference to sin it signifies "to take away," as in Rom. 6:6, "that our body of sin might be done away with, that we should no longer be slaves to sin" (NASB). John's first letter makes it very clear: "The Son of God appeared for this purpose, that He might destroy the works of the devil" (3:8, NASB), of which the carnal nature is prime ground.

2. Language Study a Guide to Clarity

Throughout the entire sweep of the Bible sin is accorded one kind of treatment only: destruction. Language study can greatly facilitate interpretation unless it overrides ideas and meanings to the extent that the purpose for which it was utilized in the first place—explicitness—is lost. For instance, in the Old Testament many figures of speech are employed to denote the act of cleansing, as in Malachi's imaginative use, "For He is like a refiner's fire and like fullers' soap. And He will sit as a smelter and purifier of silver, and He will purify the sons of Levi and refine them like gold and silver" (3:2-3, NASB). As a contrite sinner, David prayed in anguish, "Purify me with hyssop, and I shall be clean; wash me, and I shall be whiter than snow" (Ps. 51:7, NASB).

Terms not found in the Bible, but not contrary to it, have been added to the pulpit diction. Note, for instance, *burn out, eradicate*, or *take out root and branch.* These terms are not specifically mentioned in the Scriptures, but in no true or functional sense are they denied, either. If we are thinking of sin's destruction, ejection, or expulsion, and we definitely are, then *root and branch* or *eradicate* do not overplay or overreach the work of cleansing.

Therefore, let us be fully aware of the effectiveness and richness of metaphorical usage. The fiery metaphors of a preacher ablaze with love did more to locate and expose the writer's carnal haunts than the learned treatises of scholarly exegetes. It was not a bookish dissertation on sin that was needed, but a flaming, dramatic touch of the Divine. The scenes flashed and the pace grew hot as the preacher declared the whole counsel of God. The author saw himself as he really was, indwelt with original sin and in full rebellion against the expressed love of God. The terms the preacher used have long since been forgotten; but what did it matter, really? The truth had reached sin's victim in transforming power.

The highest commendation can be ascribed to scholarship, industry, and progress as safeguards in the transit of divine truth. But the main thrust is to get the truth to dying men and women, and God is not confined to human excellence alone. He may even accept a lesser degree of precision in scholarship to get the strong devotion and commitment the victory may demand. However, no one should take the exception suggested here as a chance to cop out on study, hard work, and excellence. No shiftless preacher is getting A's with God. And it is very likely that his report card is not causing any jubilation in the congregation, either.

In the intricate diversity and beauty of the 119th psalm, "Keep his way pure" (v. 9, NASB) is abridged in the literary medium of prose where a young man's plea is transparently clear: his need is cleansing. In his vision of the Most High a painful light fell upon his youthful, yet sinful, heart. Isaiah repeated his agony when he cried out, "Woe is me, for I am ruined! Because I am a man of unclean lips . . . ; for my eyes have seen the King, the Lord of hosts" (6:5, NASB). It was moral encounters with God that caused the fearful lacks to show up. But now in the Father's goodwill the young man could close his plea, "I shall delight in Thy statutes; I shall not forget Thy word" (Ps. 119:16, NASB).

3. *Study Sheds Light on Basic Truths*

The clarity increases as we advance from Testament to Testament and from book to book that the trilogy of redemption pervades the divine-human encounter as it goes forward through history. Symbol and reality are linked; promise and realization merge in one life-style, a Christ-centered walk. Thus, the Christian narrative of redemption is not a rationally joined catenation of "moments" and "mighty acts" that the neoorthodoxists variously teach.[19]

No longer a vaulted metaphysical reflection, the Highest touched the earth in gracious humiliation. The only Son of God himself walked among men. The Hebrews scribe caught the image powerfully, "For surely it is not angels he helps, but Abraham's descendants. For this reason he had to be made like his brothers in every way, in order that he might become a merciful and faithful high priest in service to God, and that he might make atonement for the sins of the people. Because he himself suffered when he was tempted, he is able to help those who are being tempted" (2:16-18, NIV).

In recent times, psychologists have had a breakthrough on the value of touching. Its salutary benefits are often helpful in simple emotional disturbances or even in psychosomatic problems. To isolate a single meaning for "touch" in the Scriptures is a highly complex undertaking, since it is used in many different ways and circumstances. Yet, there is a common denominator implied, and it falls in the area of influence and communication. "Touch" is God's expression for bringing His influence to bear in any happening, whether concrete or intangible, having in mind communication. Touching has become an integral part in many Christian fellowships, for it gives an awareness of belonging.

Very unfortunately, the beautiful, warm expression of touching can become, by the wily conniving of charlatans, a panacea of physical and emotional stimulation which may lead to imprudent evil ends. The trusting, but unwary, saint needs to be forewarned against indiscreet touching under all circumstances. If the touch does not point to and encourage holiness and purity of thought and deed, it should be avoided at all cost, even the loss of supposed friendship! Otherwise, its aftermath can amount to a psychological disaster.

The Ancient of Days literally touched the earth with redemption when He sent His only begotten Son to die on Calvary. The effectiveness of that touch is not in its magic or charm words, but in its power to transform. When the power of the Eternal Christ in some real sense touches the sinner, he is changed; behold, "he is a new creature" (2 Cor. 5:17). And, as surely, when in a second crisis the Holy Spirit touches the Father's child and cleanses him from inbred sin, his love is perfected and he then loves "with a pure heart fervently" (1 Pet. 1:22).

Thus, in holy accord, holiness undergirds and interrelates the gospel promise and endeavor of the New Testament, and in living reality fulfills the Old Testament as a prophetic and inspired covenant. It focuses in the inseparable oneness of which Christ speaks in His high-priestly prayer, "I have given them the glory that you gave me, that they may be one as we are one" (John 17:22, NIV).

> Lord, Thou hast made thyself to me
> A living, bright reality;
> More present to faith's vision keen
> Than any outward object seen;
> More dear, more intimately nigh
> Than e'en the closest earthly tie.
>
> (AUTHOR UKNOWN)

As Metz states it, "The history of redemption is the history of God's endeavor to impart His own nature, His holiness, to man. The biblical revelation leaves no doubt that holiness is the focal point of redemptive history."[20]

F. F. Bruce correctly exalts the good news of the gospel above the naturalism, or more definitely humanism, of Plato and his teacher, Socrates, whose metaphysical thinking and code of ethics are models of ancient rationalism, further refined by the trenchant thinking of Aristotle, Plato's protégé, in the *Nichomachean Ethics*. Bruce's lucid rebuttal capably counters Greek dualism: "The Christian gospel is not primarily a code of ethics or a metaphysical system; it is first and foremost good news, and as such it was proclaimed by the earliest preachers."[21] He adds further, "And this good news is intimately bound up with the historical order, for it tells how for the world's redemption God entered into history, the eternal came into time, the kingdom of heaven invaded the realm of earth, in the great events of the incarnation, crucifixion, and resurrection of Jesus the Christ."[22]

Paul's letter to the Colossians throws light on the descent of Deity in history: "Even the mystery which hath been hid from ages and from generations, but now is made manifest to his saints: to whom God would make known what is the riches of the glory of this mystery among the Gentiles; which is Christ in you, the hope of glory" (1:26-27).

E. Trilogy of Redemption in Review

The trilogy of redemption is not random, vagrant probing in search of truth. On the contrary, it is creative foreknowing, heralding the glad tidings of blessed and real things to come. *Obey*, *love*, and *cleanse* as main lines of the Old Testament pervade the New Testament in due time, making real the trailblazing of Deity as He advances unerringly through history, actuating His great plan of redemption. The remarkable undertaking in its full import is for God to touch the finite creature with His holiness and thus transform him, making him like Himself.

In any event, the path of holiness through the Scriptures is clear, undefiled, and undeviating. There need be no problem beyond solution in an honest attempt to trace it, conform to it, and proclaim it. *Obey, love, cleanse* are the main-line principles diffused throughout God's written revelation. Intrinsic and constitutional in the Old Testament, the trilogy of redemption, without moral alteration, moves into the New Testament where the window opens on reality. Love pours like a river off the arms of Calvary to engulf a sin-ridden world. It is a whosoever-will-may-come summons with no restrictions on account of race, nation, or creed. All men are debtors to its prevenient outreach, its loving concern. Every creature of Adam's race is within the bounds of its "blessed assurance, Jesus is mine." In the yielded believer, Calvary's cascade of love is "poured out within our hearts through the Holy Spirit who was given to us" (Rom. 5:5, NASB).

Indwelling love now pursues the course so extensively and pervasively begun in the Old Testament; holiness inhabits man! The graveclothes of symbol and law are laid aside, and Resurrection power breaks out of the tomb; the Redeemer is alive forevermore, and believers share richly in His inheritance.

2

Preaching Holiness

DOCTRINALLY

So the word of the Lord to them will be,
"Order on order, order on order,
Line on line, line on line,
A little here, a little there."
Isa. 28:13, NASB

The Holy Scripture is the plenary revelation of God to man in relation to his redemption.

In that the fulfillment of God's intent and plan for salvation depends on man's understanding grasp of His message and basic purpose, too much emphasis cannot be placed on the anatomy and accessibility of that divinely inspired communication. Salvation is by faith alone, but understanding is by daily experience in salvation.

At all cost, the highest degree of understanding possible must be associated with the receiving of the saving grace of God by faith. Not only need saving truth be vividly real in a crisis experience, but a framework of reference is needed by the child of God to guide his steps as he walks the holy way; thus, doctrine provides a learning experience to augment and make clear where possible the believer's saving experience.

A. Framework of Doctrine Essential

Conflicting countercultures call for intelligent discernment, especially when communication is the object. The saturation point in culture exchange seems almost reached in this day of technology eclipse in the modus operandi. The surpassing wonders of technology call all cultures into account, "for when the technology of communication changes, there is a concomitant change in the culture's way of perceiving reality," according to Paul Brooks, school communications, Fort Worth, Tex.[1] He adds further, "The church is not in the business of entertainment, but of teaching and training in biblical truths and principles."

The answer to "Why a theology?" is now evident: because teaching and training presuppose structure and system. Doctrine is Bible teaching reduced to primary principles to aid in instruction and understanding. In doctrine the believer has an orderly approach to the Scriptures, which otherwise to him would be incoherent expression. The Bible is not methodized theology, nor is it the happy hunting ground of text-grabbing zealots. It is prophecies, records, pronouncements, proverbs, and songs with no systematic linkage proposed. This does not mean that no obvious bonds of relation exist in the Bible; for one thing, the long arms of prophecy and promise properly understood bind it securely. A way for searching out those bonds for intelligent grouping and study is necessary if experience is to mean anything, and that discipline is called theology.

A systematic doctrinal pattern can forestall the danger of vague wanderings from the Word of God and from logic. "Pure reason" robbed Kant of rational ground for God. Indeed he had a god but only by postulation, along with freedom and immortality. He is reason's beacon of history; no brighter light ever shone along the shore of time, yet all that is really left of his toil is doubt and skepticism as his reward. Hence, the God who exists in revelation, not reason, becomes the axis of thought for any dependable system of thinking. Speculation has plundered the church's housetop view of existence and reality, but a comprehensive study of the Bible brings us back to a divine plan and its human fulfillment.

Theology comes from the Greek words *theos* (deity) and *logos* (discourse) and deals with the existence and nature of God. However, its meaning and use have been broadened until it becomes a systematic study of all issues related to God, man, and the plan of salvation. It is in the larger context that *theology* is used herein.

Doctrine, perhaps more than anything else, assures stability, for it tends to counter insidious drift. Abandonment and drift are of the same fabric, really; only time makes the difference. That which conduces to drift, whether subtle or evident, ends in the throes of hopeless abandonment. One moves readily to the words of Timothy L. Smith, speaking in a 1979 leadership conference, in which with God-given insight he laid down the elements of compromise which led "historic Methodism away from its Wesleyan mission."[2] As a forewarning, Dr. Smith noted especially "the willingness to accept the adequacy of ministers whose quest for Christian perfection had not yet led them into the experience of perfect love." To lack the experience of perfect love plants a dangerous shift at the very foundation of preaching, which brings apace the sad truth of Smith's observance.

All Bible teaching eventuates in doctrine. The quip that "we don't believe in teaching doctrine" begs the question; not to believe in teaching doctrine is in itself a doctrine. (Perhaps *dogma* would be more suitable at that point.) It is not whether we will teach doctrine or not—we will, if we

teach—but the emphasis should fall rather on the doctrines we teach, whether they are biblical, sound, and livable.

If we teach holiness scripturally and effectively, we will teach it doctrinally. The term *doctrine* is used to signify a form of instruction that is systematic, structuralized, and coherent. Apart from doctrine and system, teaching tends to be piecemeal, a dangerously unorganized collection of sayings, idioms, private experiences, opinions, and chitchat, usually related only by chance to the deeper things of God's Word. Thus, sound, biblically endowed doctrine makes good insurance against ministerial nomadism in the pulpit.

An alarm bell rang clearly from T. E. Martin, who stated that it was Paul's conviction "that preaching doctrine was redemptive both for the preacher and the hearer."[3] Hence, sound doctrine magnifies the pulpit and it fortifies the pew. The entire church body and movement are elevated and strengthened in the afterglow.

The preacher who meekly proposes that he will preach the Word, not doctrine, is really more sanctimonious than sound. By any measure of comparison, the Bible holds priority over anything else for preaching reference; in fact, it has no true rival. But the point in question is not a problem of precedence—Which shall come first? Rather, Where does it lead to in bringing about the most valid insights regarding the Scriptures?

Doctrine does not, and must not, replace the Bible. Doctrines biblically oriented are lines of communication between God's mind and man's in an intelligent disclosure of truth. God is an intelligent person, and He created man in His image. God deals with His creature morally and intellectually. The moral quality we call holiness, the intelligent transmission of His truth we call doctrine.

Richard S. Taylor stresses the indispensability of doctrine. He asserts, "It is because correct doctrine is so indispensable that Paul commands the preacher: 'Hold fast the form of sound words' (2 Tim. 1:13); and, 'Take heed unto . . . the doctrine . . . for in doing this thou shalt both save thyself, and them that hear thee' (1 Tim. 4:16)."[4] Paul further warns Timothy in his second letter concerning the failure to teach sound doctrine: "For the time will come when they will not endure sound doctrine; but wanting to have their ears tickled, they will accumulate for themselves teachers in accordance to their own desires" (4:3, NASB). Paul also cautions that error is not passive, for those who will not endure sound doctrine "will turn away their ears from the truth, and will turn aside to myths" (v. 4, NASB).

Biblically illuminated, a message should be the pride and joy of the minister, for a sermon well pointed with scriptural references is, as John Keats esthetically put it, "a thing of beauty and a joy forever; its loveliness increases; it will never pass into nothingness."[5]

B. Experience Essential in Preaching Holiness

Even though doctrine is imperative in preaching holiness, the effective preaching of holiness begins in experience. Doctrine cannot replace personal experience. The preacher's own heart aglow with holy incandescence is the unique precedent for a ministry of holiness preaching. On that account, we must start the doctrinal study of holiness in relation to preaching at the point of the preacher's personal experience in holiness.

Holiness is not a body of knowledge, like science, which can be put together and then taught to others. The fault of Socrates comes to mind: "Virtue is knowledge, and can be taught." Scientific knowledge results from intelligently sorting, classifying, and arranging facts available to all observers. Probable conclusions are induced and deduced from the observed data after one or more hypotheses are struck. Further tests tend to insure greater validity, but no test yet known to man can give certainty or lay claim to the absolute. It is for this reason that science cannot ascertain spiritual truth.

Holiness obtains in an intimate experience with God, a purifying and firing of the seeker's heart, which becomes the fountainhead of true holiness preaching. No station stop short of full salvation, with its two qualifying crisis experiences, prepares the preacher for his high calling, his holy task.

As Barclay puts it succinctly, "The call of God is not simply a wide, general call to all mankind; it is God's personal summons and invitation to each individual man. God does not only purpose the salvation of all mankind, he has 'His own secret stairway into every heart.' He invites each man individually to respond to Him."[6] By that "secret stairway" a meaningful spiritual intimacy must be kept alive and well.

1. Experience Is Touching Reality

The Christian religion is not a code, it is a life. In experience man touches God; God and man exchange responses and establish reciprocal relations. Man responds to God's requirement, "Thy will be done," and God responds to man's need, bestowing the Holy Spirit in His fullness. All territory comes under one sovereignty, the will and sway of Calvary's Conqueror. Thus, holiness is God incarnate in man, the fulcrum and mainstay of everything. He must experience and know God consciously and really. He must be imbued, moved, and directed by a power better than his own.

If sinners and believers ever get in touch with reality, then the minister must by all odds be aflame with God's Holy Spirit. Both his words and deeds in the pulpit and outside of it will miss the mark if his own soul misses reality. Experience is the open door to reality, and the Word of God is the living Guide; it is the touchstone to sound, knowledgeable preaching of holiness. Eloquence or dramatics cannot make up for the visible lack of self-confidence on the part of the preacher when he himself is not fully persuaded.

2. Experience Is Knowledge

Believe it or not, a preacher standing in the pulpit shining with "blessed assurance" will get the truth to listeners with greater success than any oracle who equivocates and zigzags ambiguously along the course, vainly trying to fit strange whims and ideas together in a theological puzzle. A fact hard for some to acknowledge is that a preacher with holiness of heart, on fire for God in an up-to-date experience, can get more believers into the Canaan triumph, holiness indwelt, than a legion of polished orators who may know everything about theology and homiletics, but know nothing by personal experience about the doctrine they are trying to expound.

However, we must not assume that this observation amounts to a scorning or rebuff of preparation for the ministry. There is little excuse, and no place, in the present day for serious lack of knowledge in presenting the gospel. We are not calling for a kite tail of college degrees to impress, but a comprehension that comes from enough study and training to meet the superior challenge of the ministry. It is not the evil of study which some ministerial candidates really try to avoid; it is the hard work and lifelong commitment it demands.

Experience, then, is a pliable, dynamic knowledge that speaks of confidence and certainty. Its absence yields naught but basic emptiness and futility; its best substitute apart from reality is shallow, insipid pretext. Let us put experience and good sense together; God did.

3. Experience Is Testimony and Witness

The holiness preacher is a witness as well as an advocate. He is a herald of the Good News, but he is more than a press agent; he is also witness to it. A witness is one who has been at the scene under question and can testify to its reality. To equivocate or show doubt at this point would likely forfeit the case. Testimony of an eyewitness receives highest rating in court. Nothing can take the place of a bona fide first-person account in search for evidence—"I was there when it happened, and I ought to know." Blessed is the messenger who can declare in the pulpit, "I know; I was there when it happened." To fail at this point is to fall into ambiguity which discourages confidence in those who hear.

Experience is the pile driver in practical, picture-window living. Peter advised, "Live such good lives among the pagans that, though they accuse you of doing wrong, they may see your good deeds and glorify God on the day he visits us" (1 Pet. 2:12, NIV). The radiance of first-person experience not only stands up in court, it stands out in our daily walk.

C. Understanding Essential to Stability and Instruction

Religious experience beyond doubt is better felt than told, more enjoyably realized than related; but if we are aiming at stability and permanent good, then we need to insure a value in its relationships, meanings, and ultimate importance.

Proceedings are often moved along in emotional bursts and jets of power, but the pitch which throws the immobile into action itself soon passes away. Emotional states come and go, moods change, and feelings often depend on conditions around us, conditions which affect us physically, mentally, and spiritually. Typically this kind of experience is in transition; it may be good or bad for us while it lasts; the only redeeming thing about it usually is that it will change. Even good feelings at prolonged high intensity strike at our balance mechanism; no one can live on "cloud nine" all the time. Nor in the best interest and welfare of the whole person should he try. That life is made up of sterner stuff, bestrewed along the way, not always conveniently, inclines the whole to a more healthful balance.

The true Christian experience does not depend on passing whimsies, pleasant feelings, or shifting moods. It may involve any, or even all, of these because it is the experience of a human being as well as a Christian. There is no need to disregard humanity in the Christian quest; why try to outdo God? He not only foreknew the deep complexity the divine-human encounter would incorporate, but He put His full sanction upon it: "And God saw all that He had made, and behold, it was very good" (Gen. 1:31, NASB). When Divinity makes community with humanity, even the common cause represented is never void of realistic traces of the human being. Jesus Christ became man in a special sense, but man in no actual way is God. Thus there is plenty of room for Pope's *bon mot*, "To err is human, to forgive, divine."[7]

Error computes rapidly when we try to eject the "human drag" as evil. In entire sanctification the crucifying dethronement of the sinful self gives full sovereignty of the heart to Christ. The believer as finite being remains unmodified, very humanly a creature, but very divinely a child of God, sanctified through and through.

The minister of the gospel is a human being; apart from his ordained office he is merely one of the flock. However, the palsy of the pew must not trademark the pulpit. At this high level, control and balance are incumbent on a preacher, else the emotional levels of the church have no safeguard.

Nonetheless, when the Spirit-filled preacher gets caught up in the intensity of his message, under the anointing of the blessed Holy Spirit he faces desperation—he must be heard, he must be understood. If the emotional pitch is stepped up, even the culture balance tipped somewhat—so what? He is on an extreme, critical mission. Preaching the dynamic gospel loads the frail human cart dangerously heavy at times. Dynamic preaching does not dishonor the pulpit; it is not dynamite but deadness that imperils the watchman's tower.

To subsume the diverse, highly individualized ministry of the holiness movement under any standard of pulpit conduct in preaching would amount to a serious affront to the work of the Holy Spirit in history. Every called-out watchman of the Cross has endowments peculiarly his own, bestowed by God and singular to his success as a servant of God. The overshadowing truth is, whatever originality he will ever express lies right here; and if he is going to be something more than a poor carbon copy of somebody else, he will need to be himself. Holiness can sustain the impact of emotion and variety, but can it reconcile the questions of a curious mind? To that issue we now turn.

1. Holiness Is Attested by the Intellect

The experiences of life, religious or otherwise, are, by the nature of man's makeup, related inseparably to his intellect and memory.

Experience makes God, holiness, and all first-person acquaintances knowable immediately or directly. Reason renders what is known in experience consistent. Hence, experience and reason are functionally incorporated in knowledge-getting.

Holiness as a life experience is an object of intellectual inquiry also. A curious mind will not rest in the presence of fallacy, prejudice, or the irrational; nor will God condemn the banishment of error from any domain. The Christian scholar accepts and is thrilled by the challenge.

The principal reason for this writing indulgence is the high, yet indispensable, place of experience in knowing and learning, specifically true in religion. It casts strong light on the essentiality of the experience of holiness in the life of the preacher who declares it. If a know-so experience of holiness is missing from the preacher's preparation, he is a powerless robot of formality when he should be a dynamic servant of faith. As empty as are Kant's concepts without the content of experience, just so empty and vain is the holiness preacher without a definite, second-crisis experience in entire sanctification. Experience makes God knowable, reason makes Him intelligible, and life makes Him practically livable.

But do we not know God by faith? Are we implying that God is only a rational concept? Indeed, we know God by faith, but believing which does not eventuate in an experience of reality is not really faith. The KJV spells out the meaning of faith as substance, as evidence, "the substance of things hoped for, the evidence of things not seen" (Heb. 11:1). However, the NIV seems to the writer to explain this knowing by faith even more simply and clearly: "Now faith is being sure of what we hope for and certain of what we do not see." Thus, faith is a way of knowing; faith makes God knowable, for faith is conscious trust in God now. Faith is not a category, that is belief. Faith is active, belief is passive. One can have a whole list of beliefs, what he holds to be true or false. Faith, however, is a doing, not a dogma; it takes place now, a present enactment.

Saving faith is the crisis of believing unto salvation, when the sinner casts himself in simple, childlike trust upon the promise of God. In a moment, in the "twinkling of an eye," the transfer is made; the penitent is forgiven and justified in an act of faith. As a fully conscious participant, the saved person is aware of what happened, and he can say with assurance, "I know."

In all likeliness, it does seem that God would communicate directly with His children. Why create man in His image, capable of intellectual interchange, otherwise? If personal communication with God is denied, the deep, underlying meaning of creation is forfeited. God had fellowship in mind when He endowed His special creature with personality, for fellowship involves forms of intelligent communication. God's people are a community of living, touching, communicating, knowing Christian saints of sound experience and intelligence. As Wesley phrased it, commenting on Rom. 8:16, witness "is an inward impression on the soul, whereby the Spirit of God directly witnesses to my spirit that I am a child of God."[8]

2. Doctrinal Structure Imperative for Study and Survival

The purpose of doctrine is to put beliefs into an accessible framework of reference.

Experience is first-person, direct, completely individual; and it cannot be shared with another, except through some means of communication. *Belief* is "a state or habit of mind in which trust or confidence is placed in some person or thing."[9] Belief may be held in common, though each one may experience slight variation on account of personal, predetermined sets.

To give personal experience social adaptability, it must be reduced to belief or doctrine. To render experience consistent, we must order and structuralize its content, whether religious or secular. Study and understanding depend on knowledge being interrelated and organized. A striking feature of all false religions is an evident lack of a clear, biblical, and practical account of God's holiness.

For alert, discriminating study, doctrine provides utility for active, organized minds. The holiness preacher puts together his thoughts, hopes, issues, and probabilities in a workable system of holy candor and holy life-style, "a vessel for honor, sanctified, useful to the Master, prepared for every good work" (2 Tim. 2:21, NASB). Doctrines are supporting guidelines, and study is a prime essential if survival is hoped for in the end.

3. Doctrine Renders Christian Experience Intelligible

Among a puzzling maze of experience and teaching the Christian must find his way.

No one puts out to sea, subject to every wind that blows, without a chart and compass. The sea voyager takes every precaution to secure his journey; so also must the voyager in spiritual navigation. God has carefully laid down man's travel plan; the lines are plainly marked in His chart, the inspired written Revelation. To discover and establish those lines is the task of the Bible theologian; when clarified and structured, they are called doctrines. The traces of Jesus Christ run throughout the Scriptures; they form a body of reference which constitutes the basis for theology and doctrine.

For that reason, holiness must be preached biblically and doctrinally, bearing the trademarks of sound exegesis and hermeneutics. All of this is the preacher's task; but for the people it has to make daylight connections and good sense. Holiness must relate intimately to the pew level if the believer is going to experience it genuinely.

If holiness survives repeated emotional letdowns, it has to be a part and parcel of thought. When a child of God reflects on the holy way and the sanctified life, he is not rebelling or doubting; actually, if he properly carries this out, he is giving depth and meaning to experience and knowledge. Only as the saint meditates on divine things, including his own situation, can intelligent perspective be gained for experience and life. Honest questioning and fatal doubt are not of the same family order; in fact, they are not blood relatives at all.

There is plenty of room for inquiry. God would not create a curious creature like man in His own image, stamp him with creativity and imagination, and then stifle and silence the very urge He had placed within him. Let us not degrade God's wise favor entrusted to the human race.

4. Doctrine Helps the Believer Find His Way

The path from the new birth to entire sanctification is beset with many unexpected problems. Even though it is basically true that the best qualification in the quest for holiness is to "hunger and thirst after righteousness" (Matt. 5:6), still the believer needs instruction and direction in the pilgrimage.

Prior to all other means, however, the best qualification in seeking God is a condition of heart and mind so vividly expressed by the Psalmist, "As the deer pants for the water brooks, so my soul pants for Thee, O God" (42:1, NASB). He continues, "My soul thirsts for God, for the living God." In the quest for righteousness, nothing can take the place of a deep soul hunger and thirst the seeker feels for God.

With or without emotional display, what matters? It is settled in the Word: "purify your hearts, ye double minded" (Jas. 4:8). At this point the author found doctrine and advice from the elders most helpful. His district superintendent reminded him, "What you need is a clean heart." That was the clue: a clean heart and not merely emotional satisfaction. The victory came and the battle was won, a battle the author had largely created by checking his emotions instead of Bible doctrine. Yet, with the blessed assurance of purification came the emotional fulfillment: "And though you have not seen Him, you love Him, and though you do not see Him now, but believe in Him, you greatly rejoice with joy inexpressible and full of glory" (1 Pet. 1:8, NASB).

A well-ordered doctrinal approach is needed by the believer as he finds his way along the Christian path to glory. He must come to see that as a human being he is fallible, subject to mistake, and in God's good grace must learn and grow. If he can see it, and accept it, as part of the divine plan, half the real battle is already won. Does not the Holy Spirit guide us perfectly? Yes, but human beings do not follow perfectly. That's the rub. How could one sin, or make a mistake, or fail, and be perfect? By the same omen that he does not follow the Holy Spirit perfectly. Calvary atones for the discrepancies; the Redeemer died for the human race.

Apart from sound doctrine the way is fraught with error and miscalculation. To say that we must die in the act of putting away the sinful self actually raises the problem of oblivion, as though the seeker had to die terminally. God's plan of redemption does not destroy the precious person-reality we call the self; sin defiled that self, but full salvation purifies it and makes it whole again. Indeed, it is death to the sinful self, but it is life and joy to the purified saint. The so-called death route is not a funeral procession to the grave of extinction; it is rather a purifying leap into dynamic life.

With prayer and disciplined learning through doctrinal instruction, the believer begins to see the light and to grasp the truth as it touches the entire compass of the Scriptures. Well-organized doctrine provides guidance for intellectual understanding in the experience and life of the believer. Wrong-headedness and pure-heartedness can be blessedly resolved, with unsound notions and error rooted out as Bible truth separates the wheat from the chaff.

5. Doctrine Establishes the Sanctified

Entire sanctification is not maturity; more realistically it is matriculation, as someone has said. Once in the experience of full salvation, the believer then needs to "grow in the grace and knowledge of our Lord and Savior Jesus Christ" (2 Pet. 3:18, NASB). Doctrines are his guideposts as he walks about the Kingdom.

Let it be remembered, in any event, doctrine is not a replacement for the Scriptures or the leadership of the Holy Spirit. On the contrary, if doctrine is biblically sound, it will aid the Holy Spirit's efforts to lead the saint into all truth: "When He, the Spirit of truth, comes, He will guide you into all the truth" (John 16:13, NASB). Further, doctrine gives the newly sanctified the benefits of the prayers, experiences, and Spirit leadings of the mature Christians.

If anyone should react to this concept of doctrine, he no doubt would do so contending that the child of God is established in sanctification, and all grace, by the Word, and not by doctrine. The writer would take no exception whatever to the thesis that a Christian is established by the Word of God in all grace. The alternative is unthinkable in that it is not only unscriptural, but it disastrously weakens the whole case by humanizing it.

However, the question is not directed to alternation; no notion of option or replacement is even hinted at. The question is not "what" establishes the believer; rather, what makes that establishment intelligible? What could apart from doctrine? Is there no design, no connected theme, no sequence, no thread of evidence in the Bible narrative? Every Bible reader and lover knows that there is; and, what is more, he depends temporally and eternally on it. The problem under study is how to find those lines of evidence, isolate them, and then relate them in a frame of investigation. How the lines of knowledge are extended to comprehend God's will and plan in relation to God's Word we routinely call doctrine.

Sanctification as a second work of grace, subsequent to the new birth, was roundly and loudly rejected by a majority rule of American churchmen. To the amazement of some of us, in recent years second blessing opponents have publicly introduced a grace stimulus for Christian believers in the form of "infillings." It does not propose baptism with the Holy Spirit or cleansing as prescribed under the Wesleyan teaching. Rather, it merely adds "infilling" to the teaching of progressive sanctification.

However, the Wesleyan concept of "the infilling" is not only true to the Word of God, but also realistic and true to life. It proposes one baptism with cleansing, followed by "infillings" as the need arises in the Christian life. "Accurately speaking, there is one baptism with the Spirit, but many subsequent refreshings, quickenings, anointings, and enduements by the Spirit for life services."[10] Infillings are, therefore, replenishment for the believer, not recovery for the backslider. The saga of Christian trial and suffering is a reminder of those heroic days when God graciously and adequately met the needs of His people with fresh anointings and assurances of His constant love and care. One baptism, but infillings many. How many? Positively no limit: "And as thy days, so shall thy strength be" (Deut. 33:25).

The safeguarding of sound doctrine can hardly be overrated when one takes a specimen study of the theology and practices of the present-day world of religion. It represents a range of beliefs and opinions spread across hundreds of denominations, sects, cults, and many nondescript groups; a hodgepodge of doctrine, dogma, religious whim, or personality quirk, conveniently related to the Bible but not founded on the harmony of God's Word.

The freedom from danger of deception cannot be

wholly eliminated, but thankfully it can be greatly reduced. As a blessed recompense, nonetheless a high degree of security can be our reward if we take care to establish believers and the entirely sanctified in the Holy Word by sound doctrine.

6. Doctrine Secures the Church Against Error

A scrupulously ordered doctrinal structure based on complete conformity to the Scriptures is life insurance for the church. Guidelines thus certified safeguard the creedal fidelity of the body. Even though the doctrinal confession may not be a fixed pattern of laws, so that there is allowance for new light and growth, its ranks can be secured only as long as its theology makes coherent scriptural sense.

Adjustment of doctrine does not imply necessary intent to abandon that doctrine, but to illuminate it and understand it better as light and knowledge increase, "and attaining to all the wealth that comes from the full assurance of understanding, resulting in a true knowledge of God's mystery, that is, Christ Himself, in whom are hidden all the treasures of wisdom and knowledge" (Col. 2:2-3, NASB). If the writer has ever been thankful for a good doctrinal grounding, it is in the present-day twilight of spiritual reality where religions abound but biblical truth seems in short supply.

Doctrine is necessary to survival; no church is stronger than its doctrinal framework grounded on the Word of God. To say that "we are Bible-centered, not doctrine-centered" is unwittingly confusing the real issue. Any theology that is truly and thoroughly Bible-centered will function only within the realm of doctrine; Christian theology is not scatter-gun drama. Instead, it is disciplined beliefs which are studied, classified, and fully organized according to the written Revelation. Then, and only then, can it become a bulwark of defense, as well as a guide, to the follower of Christ in the war of words or the whitewash of cheap peace: "And they have healed the wound of My people slightly, saying, 'Peace, peace,' but there is no peace" (Jer. 6:14, NASB).

7. Doctrine Facilitates Study and Teaching

However one may go about Bible study, one thing is immovable—the Word, itself, is first in line. In whatever way the honest researcher explores its profound and providential depths, his first debt is to the Book. By no means can the integrity of the Word be set aside. Without exception the empiricism of science and the rationalism of philosophy must not supplant the Bible or fill in for the Living Word.

What light science can cast on Bible history—and it is not scant—is not frowned upon. That the logical principles of philosophy may be brought to bear on the manifold of historical religion is counted on for consistency in thought. So long as the normal, curious human mind pursues accuracy and fidelity, any other course is improbable. However, to suggest either or both of these as a substitute for Spirit-motivated research as a special field is a clear case of reverse discrimination. The empirical test of science cannot replace the simple act of faith, and reason by no degree of allowance can stand in for it either. They are ingenious skills of excellence in their particular fields, but they lack the field understanding and spiritual sensitivity assigned to religion.

The aim of study is understanding and consistency. Knowledge must have depth, range, and coherence and be rendered intelligible. Doctrine proposes to arrange Bible truths in a cohesive framework so that what is believed can be studied and taught. The heart of effective teaching, also preaching, is clarity and consistency. This is obviously impossible apart from structuralized belief. H. Orton Wiley, past senior theologian, sanctioned with strong emphasis the doctrinal approach to teaching as given by another prominent theologian, Charles Hodge. [11] In other words, it seems by the very nature of his being intelligent, man is made for doctrine; at least, he tends to put ideas together consistently so that he can make some sort of clearheadedness out of fact-finding and scholarship. He cannot think apart from well-coordinated ideas and judgments.

Richard Taylor seems to have cast doctrine in its proper light: "We may have doctrine without salvation, but we cannot have salvation without doctrine. If we are saved by faith, we must have something to believe, and it must be the truth. We are not saved by believing error. Jesus said, 'If ye continue in my word . . . ye shall know the truth [that's doctrine], and the truth shall make you free' (that's doctrine become experience)." [12]

To keep the shorelines of salvation and hope in view and intact, safe for any earnest wayfarer of the Cross, Bible theology, tendered in clear doctrine, is the best possible warranty for both the saint and the Church.

Preaching Holiness

EVANGELISTICALLY

Now may the God of peace Himself sanctify you entirely; and may your spirit and soul and body be preserved complete, without blame at the coming of our Lord Jesus Christ.

Faithful is He who calls you, and He also will bring it to pass.

1 Thess. 5:23-24, NASB

What do we mean when we say that we must preach holiness evangelistically?

The idea may fall into misleading speculation unless it is prayerfully and thoughtfully adapted to the present-day religious scene. So loose and illusive are the methods of evangelism in the many denominational and independent focal centers today, any attempt to reduce the hodgepodge of forms and techniques to a general pattern of action overwhelms the imagination.

Need holiness evangelism lose its identity because of widespread confusion and error? Is it not valid and impartial to assume that preaching holiness evangelistically is as sound as any other evangelistic form? To take flight in the face of perplexity and conflict is not the historical ideal and response of the holiness movement. It has recognized and worked out the flaws in its methods as they have surfaced in its resplendent progress. It is in the crisis-process context of entire sanctification that evangelism provides special facility, as we shall see later.

A. What Is Holiness Evangelism?

Stripped to the spiritual quick, holiness evangelism implies no more, no less than helping a believer into, and through, the crisis of entire sanctification. Whatever means and ways are involved are not as important as the actual experience of being sanctified. It matters little how much we may prefer one method over another, or even if we should question the use of any specific method; there should be no disagreement regarding the critical need of the believer "getting through" to a genuine experience in entire sanctification itself.

Dr. Paul R. Orjala notes the "growing hunger and search for a deeper spiritual life," then prescribes the answer as "massive commitment to holiness evangelism." In the ensuing discussion, Dr. Orjala proposes a definition of holiness evangelism: "a clear, simple definition which I believe we need at this present time. . . . Holiness evangelism is getting people sanctified, just as basic evangelism is getting people saved," he continues. Certainly that is an unadorned, workaday definition, to be sure, but in it Dr. Orjala strikes the main chord of our need. His meaning comes through with greater clarity when he adds, "The goal of holiness evangelism is to get people sanctified—not just to study it, not just to proclaim it—as important as these activities are in moving toward the goal."[1]

B. Crisis and the Vital Change

However the course of action may go, one thing is imperative, and that is the crucial moment when the vital change takes place in the believer's heart and he is sanctified wholly. Attendance of crisis increases the inevitable need of decision; it is brought on to incite the believer to act. The verdict, a willed act, is the purpose and objective of the crisis. Evangelism serves to expedite the crisis, to bring it on and to sustain it. In the crisis the believer tends to take the needed step of faith in a critical surrender when he claims God's promise, and the victory is won.

If we were to restrict evangelism exclusively to saving sinners, then we would separate it from its significant place in history. Evangelism has served all the spiritual needs of the church and the community. Sinners were saved, a phase known as *evangelism;* and the believers were sanctified, building and strengthening the church, an aspect generally referred to as *revival.* However, these were not separate or distinct forms, but complements of the major thrust, or campaign, called simply evangelism or revival.

Oddly enough, some of the worst sinners have been saved while the preacher stressed holiness, and some of the nicest believers have experienced sanctification while he preached on hell. Do not ask why it is that way. Larry Hanson testified to me that in a revival service in Waltham, Mass., he could hardly wait until the sermon on judgment was over so that he could go to the altar and get sanctified. Some of the best evangelistic results have followed strong, biblical preaching on holiness, for it creates a holy climate charged with incentive. To cite Dr. Orjala again, "The curious enigma is that we have always done a better job of basic evangelism (getting people saved) when we have had a strong focus on holiness evangelism (getting people sanctified)."[2]

Believers hunger and thirst for full salvation, thence the believer's inducement to be wholly sanctified as an essential part of the living stream of salvation. Actually, holiness evangelism is the process which brings the believer's spiritual urge to blessed fruition. As Peter apprehended it in his First Epistle, "Like newborn babies, crave pure spiritual milk, so that by it you may grow up in your salvation, now that you have tasted that the Lord is good" (2:2-3, NIV).

C. Subjective Longing Crucial

The writer questions whether sufficient emphasis is being placed on the subjective longing of the believer in his quest. "Hunger," "thirst," or "panting" are not emotional states worked up at the moment. Perhaps it could be adduced as a consummate longing that the believer has to be one with God and to do His perfect will. To "pant" for fulfillment and completion in Christ is better than "standing pat" on doctrinal issues. Thirst and longing will bring the seeker and Christ together more quickly and effectively than anything else.

The redemption story is replete with struggle and endeavor toward the best, however one may feel about the term *perfection*. In this commitment of man's will, surrender to God must be complete, and it is total. God is not on trial. It is all out or it is all off. No middle ground is even alluded to in the vast Bible compass. Nor does it hint at anything like a graduated scale of bargaining and compromise. The best theology regarding the experience is expressed in the old altar-call song, "I Surrender All."

Entire surrender must precede entire sanctification. At this point a crisis obtains, and two wills meet—God's and man's. In order to bring the process to completion in perfect love, the divine will must have the believer's unqualified sanction; it is not a test run, a venture to test or prove God's integrity; it is forever. Then that forever act ends the crisis of entire sanctification, and love is made perfect (complete).

The realization of completion in entire sanctification does not terminate the process of sanctification; a specific work was achieved as the love shed abroad in the believer's heart at the new birth was perfected (completed). The sanctifying process continues on through the new birth and entire sanctification, perhaps into eternity. It depends altogether on how broadly one defines the term. The writer prefers not to be caught up in idle argumentation that is not profitable; so while recognizing the possibility and value of sanctification as separation in its wider use, he has adopted the idea that sanctification begins in the new birth and continues on to completion, or perfection, in the crisis step of entire sanctification. Not that such a position is without argumentative challenge, but it is Wesleyan and functional.

In the far-reaching sense, sanctification begins wherever God intercepts the sinner on his wayward journey. It then continues progressively through two moral experiences or crises—the new birth and entire sanctification—and on to the glory world. Respecting the benevolent reality of prevenient grace at every point of concern, no attempt will be made to put God within bounds not prescribed morally.

Whereas the journey may be long and rugged, the seeker is greatly encouraged and spurred on by an insatiable longing for God and cleansing from sin, a craving hunger and thirst as compelling as the deer panting for the brook. As a love suit, the emotional drive is a ruling factor and needs prayerful care and consideration; it must be satisfied, which means fulfillment. May the writer ask again, Is sufficient emphasis being placed on subjective longing as one of the living, dynamic means?

D. God Takes the Initiative

If we are going to talk about salvation for the human race, where shall we start the quest? Does God initiate the process, or is that man's prerogative? The point must not be circumvented, for the movement and outcome of redemption are linked unalterably to the answer. Hence, evangelism as a concept and means must confront the question. According to William Barclay, the supposed conflict between God's wrath and Paul's gospel, wherein Paul succeeds in setting the love and grace of Christ over against the wrath and austerity of God's judgment to withstand it, is in "reverse of the truth." He maintains, "If one thing is clear, it is that, to Paul, the whole initiative of the process of salvation lies with God." He adds, "It was the love of God which was behind the whole process of salvation."[3]

In John's First Epistle the redemptive concern and direction are vividly set down: "Not that we loved God, but that He loved us and sent His Son to be the propitiation for our sins" (4:10, NASB). Thus, the search was launched in the compassionate love of God; no other position could be biblically, theologically, or philosophically sound, as the writer sees it. John's direct pronouncement settles the biblical answer: It was "that He loved us and sent His Son" which secures the sinner's hope. Love has invaded the world by choice and not by invitation.

It makes a total difference whether God is seeking man or man is seeking God, initially. The quest takes its character, cadence, and, without doubt, its consummation in relation to a carefully defined polarity. In conservative theology God is seeking man; in liberal theology man is seeking God, not so much for moral recovery as for rational justification. A god-idea is almost always found indispensable to the liberal in any logical system based on ethics.

Nicolia Hartmann attacked medieval supernaturalism and the various forms of theism and founded an ethical system on philosophic humanism, the idea being: God is not necessary in ethical thinking or system building. For the liberal thinker the need is for a god that will fit comfortably into a modus operandi characterized by reasoning. Karl Barth defines religion as man's search for God, as distinguished from revelation, which is God's search for man.[4]

The conservative fancies no such predicament as the liberal encounters; God is not only the mighty Creator of all things, He is in succeeding good sense also the great Caretaker. In this simple philosophy, the conservative believes with every hallmark of logic that God is creative and positive, hence redemptive. He preserves and increases His redemptive relations within the world by any deed or demand placed upon him.

As Chester Wilkins observes, "The day of personal evangelism is here. . . . The layman must have a more important part in the program for advancement of the church."[5] All church members are ministers sent of God. Thus, God takes the initiative; He seeks the fallen creature. A theology which begins the quest for redemption at the human extreme of disadvantage is a polar miscarriage, as the Word of God unmistakably brings to view. "We love him, because he *first* loved us" (1 John 4:19, italics added). Beyond question, our love is response, not provocation. Only as we see God moving in compassionate love to our rescue do principles and practices fall into place, giving us a workable plan of redemption.

God is seeking man. There can be no biblical or reasonable appeal from this blessed truth, nor is there ever need for it. And, what is even more awe-inspiring, that holy aggressiveness extends to every detail of man's present and final salvation!

E. God's Mood and Method

To the wholly sanctified, law is neither a harsh enslavement of the human will nor an exhausted, outmoded code of ethical behavior. Rather, it is by divine implanting the new direction within the child of God himself: "Thy law is within my heart" (Ps. 40:8). Paul catches it in summary: "Being manifested that you are a letter of Christ, cared for by us, written not with ink, but with the Spirit of the living God, not on tablets of stone, but on tablets of human hearts" (2 Cor. 3:3, NASB). The highest law is full commitment; it is also the least. Love can tolerate no other standard, and love makes the law a delight, as the Psalmist declared, "I delight to do Thy will, O my God" (40:8, NASB).

Yet the concept of God as merely love can miss the mark unless love is correctly defined. If love is regarded as soft and sentimental, or amenable and comfortable, we will need to check God's Word with earnest care; somewhere something surely has gone wrong. True, Paul brings to mind, "Love is patient, love is kind . . . bears all things . . . endures all things" (1 Cor. 13:4, 7, NASB); but love as mediator is thoroughly exacting in the realm of morals; God does not wink at wee, pocket-size sins, so-called. James speaks candidly and deftly to the case: "For whoever keeps the whole law and yet stumbles in one point, he has become guilty of all" (2:10, NASB).

Situationism in ethics hits the bull's-eye, but checked in at the wrong firing range! It holds that love is for people, that we are not to love principles, a bull's-eye to be sure. But unfortunately it claims that moral quality is nominal, not real, largely in the vein of Occamism, which rejected the Thomistic concept of intrinsic moral quality. Hence, ethics and the quality are both extrinsic. "The situational-personal ethic, in short, subordinates principles to circumstances and the general to the particular," explains Robert L. Cunningham.[6] On this firing range, where there seems to be more trees than woods, unmarried love could be more moral than married love if circumstances dictate it. One wonders by what principle the nonprincipled act is judged.

It is the old, time-worn battle of the absolutes, which

some so vehemently and passionately reject. On a train trip, a little lassie who had gone to several finishing schools and had dropped out to get a taste of the "real" world was acting as stewardess on the train. We struck up a conversation; she had an interesting background but was unyielding in her views. In the course of conversation, I introduced Jesus Christ as the Answer to her admittedly mixed-up life. She turned on me and glared, snapping sharply, "Don't pull any absolutes on me; I reject the Jesus absolute."

To which I quietly replied, "I teach logic, Becky, and you have just pulled one of your absolutes on me—that there are no absolutes." Not logic but where the absolutes roost at night seems to be the answer, so I keep one handy: "It is the absolute to reject all absolutes."

Love is the most exacting of all principles; it needs no excuse to leave dark, irrelevant areas undisclosed. It seeks one thing mainly, perfection. Whenever God's love enters, it soon becomes evident that nothing short of entire sanctification is feasible or fitting; not until the whole person is spiritually whole and healthy can the ideal be fulfilled. Love may bear less than the best, but it cannot rest until the best is realized. And the best, as we have maintained, is perfect love, the effectual completion experienced in entire sanctification. What the ceremony and law could not do with their rigid disciplines, love achieved, not by destroying the law but by transcending it in delightful consecration.

In the Sermon on the Mount, Jesus moved swiftly to reassure the disciples, "Do not think that I have come to abolish the Law or the Prophets; I have not come to abolish them but to fulfill them" (Matt. 5:17, NIV). Law, rule, principle, or whatever we may call it, love is definitely more clear-cut and explicit in the tests of life, for it can search the heart with deadly precision to lay bare even the slightest flaw. In that acutely real sense, love is more exacting than law, but grace transforms law into delight, so the Psalmist could say:

> You have made known to me the path of life;
> you will fill me with joy in your presence,
> with eternal pleasures at your right hand.
>
> *(16:11, NIV)*

God's mood is love, enduring, endearing. It holds the needy and suffering in sympathy and the carnal and arrogant in pity; it is tender and entreating always. Still because of its purity, being wholly undefiled, love is explicit to the letter and unequivocal; openness, fairness, and precision mark its presence. As one would anticipate, God's method fits His mood and makes possible its fulfillment. God's method is constituted in and worked out through the strong divine urges inherent in His love. When temporal means are used, tokens of human understanding and skill, God adjusts the whole procedure to involve and employ whatever is available, but not at the price of waning or declining love. Love cannot be diluted or altered without temporal and terminal loss. Hence, while God's love is fulfilled in His method, it is equally true that His method never forsakes His love; it must remain divinely pure and holy.

F. The Believer Needs the Evangelistic Urge

Why holiness evangelism? Evangelism provides the stipulation, the direction, and the urge to get sanctified. Why do sinners come to Christ under the preaching of holiness? The answer is quite obvious; the ideal in salvation is the same for sinner or believer, namely to be Christlike. One difference obtains, however: The believer certainly has greater light and incentive to reach that blessed ideal. As the sinner needs the spur to be saved, normally called conviction, the believer needs the press to be sanctified; little is gained apart from some prod to get action, call it what we may.

If a believer has been genuinely saved, his deepest yearning (panting) is to be like Jesus. Paul's affirmation is helpful: "Therefore, if anyone is in Christ, he is a new creation; the old has gone, the new has come!" (2 Cor. 5:17, NIV). Not a rebellious sinner but a new person seeks entire sanctification. He is still carnal, but he is not Christless; though the sin of Adam besets him, the "panting" love for Christ planted in his heart in the new birth draws him to the Redeemer.

Henceforth, as a sequel to the new birth, the urge for entire sanctification copes with two main problems: an internal yearning strong enough to consummate the quest, and a vital relation in the evangelistic form adequate to carry it out.

Longing and method are adjusted to the circumstances at hand. Hard and fast rules which work well at one time and in one place prove rather awkward and ill-suited when new, different situations are faced. For instance, the writer did not employ American camp-meeting evangelistic methods in far-off India, where culture and condition completely reverse the American style. The approach, the message, and the altar appeal were by necessity quite different. How do you approach a raw, suspicious Hindu crowd which scorns and abhors the Christian way? Do you just get up and take a text and launch into your message? And do you tell them that the altar is now open, and anybody who needs Christ should come? Hardly. It has to be a religious diplomacy geared to them to allay their suspicion, to meet their need through Christ, and to bring a decision to accept Jesus as Savior. Ask any missionary, and he or she will tell you how delicate and skillful the overture must be.

Hence, longing and method are adjusted to the circumstance at hand. It has been the writer's observation that believers of all denominations "pant for the brook" of entire sanctification, whether they realize it or not. Their hearts long for more of God and His grace. Through extensive contact with believers, nationally and internationally, he finds there is adequate evidence that God's people, regardless of church affiliations, tend to make an all-out effort to please the Lord and do His will. They leave not a stone unturned to effect union with Him at whatever level of understanding they possess.

The target is to get the blessing; means and methods can be adjusted to suit the particular case. Some of the most outstanding instances of entire sanctification in the writer's own experience and ministry show clearly that method and stance are not the main ingredients in seeking entire sanctification. For instance, believers were sanctified wholly while they listened to a message on holiness, and some were sanctified on their way to the altar. The writer's former pastor was sanctified while riding on the back of a meat wagon in downtown Sault Ste. Marie, Mich. He had gone to the altar the night before in a revival service. But right there in the street, far from any religious sanctuary, he believed God's promise, and the blessing came upon him in cleansing and perfect love.

In Elizabeth, Pa., in an afternoon service during a revival series, after the writer had preached on entire sanctification, a large, well-groomed lady came up to him at the altar and asked, "Do you know what happened to me while you were preaching?" Her answer came readily, "I have been a member of a church for 45 years, taught Sunday School classes, held all the major offices, but never before today did I know that I could be sanctified instantaneously. I was so hungry; and as you preached the Word, I sat and listened, lost in prayer and thought. You made it so clear that it came by faith, I said to myself, I guess that is my next step. I knew I was saved. While I listened and finally surrendered, I was so lifted in God's wonderful Spirit and love, I just took that next step, believed God with all my heart, and right there while the service was in progress the Holy Spirit sanctified me wholly." What a happy finder! What a time of rejoicing we had!

Another instance is cited here to show that a long, holiness background is not needed if the believer is sincere. In India, a native nurse, described by Dr. Cox, the station's missionary physician, as one of the most intelligent and able Indian nurses he had ever met, was blessedly sanctified while the writer preached in a victorious Sunday morning service. Her experience told after service was that she was "panting" and thirsting as she listened to the message on entire sanctification. At a moment of full commitment and surrender she said she lifted her heart to God in simple, trusting faith, and the Holy Spirit came in His fullness; perfect love flooded her soul. She was engulfed with joy and peace. "Heaven came down and glory filled my soul" was her glad and knowing witness.

The side effects or benefits in preaching holiness are many; the victorious "fallout" touches every human need. When the Holy Spirit "falls," so to speak, on a service, believers are sanctified to be sure, but sinners are saved, God's people are uplifted and blessed, and the sick are healed. In the aforementioned service in India, when entire sanctification was the emphasis, a Hindu railroad passenger station manager was converted to Christ. A reference to the brief history of the Wesleyan movement will show that the preaching of holiness has been the prime focal point for the mighty release of the power and work of the Holy Spirit.

Such landmarks established by our fathers should not be removed, as the Proverbs remind us, "Do not move the ancient boundary" (23:10, NASB). The KJV translates it to read "old landmarks," whereas TEV gives it in paraphrase: "Never move an old property line or take over land owned by orphans." "Landmark" or "property line" is not the withering vista of an outlived tradition. They are marks which have never lost their meaning; only rock fences to be sure, but a lasting reminder of justice, peace, and honor. Once removed from the present scene, the voice of the ages is silenced, and the eternal tends to lapse away into the temporal reform. The old "property lines" are gradually sacrificed to convenience; the holy purpose for which they stood faces immediate jeopardy and, no doubt, eventual dissipation.

G. Method in Holiness Evangelism

The foregoing heads up problems in seeking entire sanctification to direct attention largely to vital, related areas complexly involved in the process. For instance, before method is considered, the author holds that it is important to have a value estimate of the seeker's subjective states, as is found in the earlier division of this chapter. Or, to advocate that God takes the initiative in seeking the well-being of all people, especially His children. Thus, the seeker in that case faces a positive situation.

The stress that has fallen on God's unchanging landmarks in the thesis of this writing points directly to the trilogy of redemption designated as obedience, love, and cleansing. These are foundational and therefore not open to change. No retrenchment from these stands can be countenanced. They are the property lines for the saint, covering the entire gamut of any full range of experience and living. Unfortunately, some have considered the landmarks of the church and God's people to be traditional customs and practices built up in the life cycle of a community. Frequently they varied from district to district, and from locale to locale, and were often found in conflict. Immediately the cry was heard, "Do not forget the landmarks." Thankfully, the true landmarks of the Bible cannot be taken captive by any particular group or community; they remain Kingdom property lines regardless of what happens to neighborhood or area differentiation.

Yet in God's dealings with the temporal world, He must find place for adjustment, which reduces to change. But how can that be? Basically because the adjustment is not a moral shift; the Holy cannot be toned down or weakened, else we have the catastrophic dilemma of the enfeebled, finite god. The person-centered philosophy of personalism presents a god weakened by the loss of omnipotence, a god limited in power, hence in future security. Not a very encouraging or inspiring prospect for the saint's quest.

The rational Greek presumed to create God in his own image, something which had not entered the mind of man before, if the Egyptians are an example of pre-Grecian worship. The earliest Greek record is in the *Iliad*, so Greek mythology began with Homer. And the change is marked. The towering colossus; the monstrous, mysterious sphinx; men with bird's heads; and lions with bulls' heads—these all fell from sight in the Greek world as reason took over and the "Greek artists and poets realized how splendid a man could be, straight and swift and strong."[7] From this supposed renaissance Plato's *Republic* and Aristotle's *Nichomachean Ethics* emerge to influence all political and ethical thought to this day; yet neither the silent sky nor the heart of questing man can communicate with old Greek rationalism which has been pretty well laid to rest in this time of superirrationalism.

In a world of inexhaustible change God's landmarks remain as immutable as God himself; thus Jesus could say, "I tell you the truth, until heaven and earth disappear, not the smallest letter, not the least stroke of a pen, will by any means disappear from the law until everything is accomplished" (Matt. 5:18, NIV). The law was in full effect until

Jesus came and fulfilled it; its effect then passed from the letter to love. But that did not lessen the effect, for love is right; it is still the essence of righteousness and integrity.

Thus, in entire sanctification the immutable and abiding join ranks with the changing temporal life of the believer, who by faith and with full awareness and consent enters into a lifelong adjustment or adaptation to the Eternal. It is a process which makes progress and growth possible in the entirely sanctified.

Useful method is worked out to handle the ongoing adjustment and fulfillment which accompany the experience of entire sanctification. The joyful believer will need further directions as he moves into the crisis and then on into the real life of entire sanctification; all along the way his soul will be crying for light. In no way is the believer trying to break down God's reluctance, but rather he seeks to submit to God's highest willingness. The believer has to adjust to bring his fragmented life into moral line with God's unchanging will. God must carry out the idea of perfection inherent in the plan of salvation from the beginning.

It is the writer's conviction that God meets the believer first at his level of understanding and competence, beginning with what knowledge he already has. Then the Holy Spirit moves gently, but firmly, to guide and encourage the endeavor. The idea that a seeker, or anyone, can manipulate God by playing on His generous sympathy is false; there are specifications to meet fully, and they are exact. While it is true that God is not a slave driver, it is equally true that He is not a weepy sentimentalist. He knows what is needed, and He knows how to get it done. Therefore, while the methods differ, and even in a few instances may disagree, seekers are getting sanctified.

Preachers alert to the problems are giving emphasis to the vital elements of entire sanctification, highlighting crisis, secondness, and growth. In the intensity of "making sure" through much of the history of the holiness movement, growth was overlooked. When the alert was sounded concerning the extra emphasis on crisis, then growth was revived and crisis began to suffer. Also, a question arose regarding the Bible support for secondness; nowhere could it be found, "This is the second experience." The negative impact shook some foundations, especially those who were not themselves in living possession of such an experience. Though the Bible does not specify, "This is it," on any particular occasions, the follow-up is obvious that there is "next after the first" in the Christian's experience of entire sanctification. The baptism with the Holy Spirit by any honest analysis is an additional grace. It was not given to sinners; and if it was an event, and it was, then it took place in crisis. That may not spell secondness, but it positively adds up to it.[8]

Biblically speaking, there is only one way to be sanctified entirely: by a full consecration and faith in the cleansing work of the Holy Spirit. But when we are referring to the seeker's way of approaching his Father, the possibilities are great, if not almost unlimited. We may prize the method employed; God prizes the soul. Dare I say it—just as there are saintly Baptists entirely sanctified in spite of their doctrine, there are also precious Nazarenes and Wesleyans sanctified in spite of our methods. Perfection in that realm is an ideal not too familiar to either fundamentalists or Wesleyans.

Two definite weaknesses hamper our approach to method. First, we tend to assume that one method works everywhere. Then, we miss the mark by taking it for granted that seeker response will be the same for everybody, everywhere.

In the first place, method as we have argued must suit the time and circumstance. On demand, we must be prepared to adjust to the new situation and use whatever method works best. In it all we are trying to bring the seeker's hope to fruition, not prove the sacredness of a method. In the second consideration, no two seekers have identical psychological sets or backgrounds, in which occurrence they have to be treated as individual cases.

Though a distinct community habit or characteristic may identify a high percentage of those living in a certain sector, exceptions to the well-known practice will show up any time under given conditions. A good, sound method will not work equally well everywhere, and unfortunately it may not work at all in some places. For that reason, method must be prayerfully adapted; method is not sacred, but souls have unparalleled worth. So, rescue souls, therefore, whatever happens to method!

In lieu of what has just been said, perhaps it should be discreetly added that method is in no wise questioned or rejected. The conforming method used to aid seekers at the altar is advised and under most circumstances urged. Care should be taken that method does not become God; it is always a means, never an end in itself. Whereas general principles do apply when seekers come to an altar, yet individual differences must be worked through and prayerfully negotiated. Often it is in the quandary of personal problems that the real issues are faced up to and coped with adequately. In the holiness movement we have developed intelligent, discerning methods in the battle for souls, and we need not be ashamed of our practices or successes. That we have faults accounts for the human element in our evangelism. Divine power released through evangelism gave birth and bearing to the vigorous, young holiness movement. For a century of time, while it has stormed the forts of evil and wickedness without break or interlude, God's mercy and dynamic have endured. Hence, it need not apologize for its toil and triumph, its shortcomings and mistakes after many decades of tireless industry. Its friends will understand; its critics will remain doubtful and suspicious in spite of everything.

Methods in holiness evangelism cover a wide range of helps and assists; some can be taught, others relate to the incident, but all must conduce to the uplift and encouragement of the sincere seeker. In a well-developed church culture of spiritual enrichment the believer is surrounded by knowledge and incentives at the proper levels of progress. The Christian church is not a monastic order, withdrawn and antisocial, with nothing more to offer the community than austerity. It is a confluence of people, all kinds of people. It is a learning center about the Word of God and His plan of salvation. The church is a place of converging cultures; everybody's upbringing goes into the crucible for sifting and refinement. The church is an emotional and social axis where friendship, work, and play mingle. All of these advantages and helps mark the normal Christian church—but they are side effects. The main objective of evangelism and soul-winning remains central and crucial in the authentic holiness church.

Preaching Holiness

PASTORALLY

For precept must be upon precept, precept upon precept; line upon line, line upon line; here
a little, and there a little.

Isa. 28:10

The pastor is the key in the proclamation of holiness, regardless of what other auxiliaries and adjuncts may be
available and in use.

The extent and depth of holiness experience and its
enjoyment in any church membership correlate vitally to
the experience and zeal of the shepherd. If his experiential
intensity and eagerness deeply motivate and excite others to
press on, holiness will grow and attract. A center of holy
love and renewing life will thus be maintained with its
power and spiritual depth.

No matter how specific, urgent, and effective the
evangelistic groundwork, unless the pastor is in constant
touch with the whole situation, and understands the need

and real joy of entire sanctification, his church will not be a holiness center.

A. Pastor the Key in Holiness Proclamation

Preparation, maturing, and seasoning in holiness are the work of the pastor. Isaiah condensed this but set down the essence of it in his expression, "Precept upon precept; line upon line, . . . here a little, and there a little." Other translators use different words or reshuffle the same ones, trying to parallel Isaiah's core meaning, which seems clear enough in all versions. The NIV offers a down-to-earth, pragmatic interpretation, "Do and do, do and do, rule on rule, rule on rule; a little here, a little there." In this particular case, a paraphrase, TEV, makes the best sense: "He is trying to teach us letter by letter, line by line, lesson by lesson."

The call here is not for a rote system, which tends to make religion a branch of knowledge largely related to the memory. It is hoped rather by Isaiah's "precept upon precept" approach we might catch a glimpse of the need for thorough study and preparation in presenting holiness, and see a distinct value in applied repetition. The intimate, vital aspects of holiness need to be recounted and retold often in a way conducive to cultivation and education. If skillfully done, this plan will not be a matter of reruns and retreads ineptly carried out to merely make a point. Painstaking effort to learn holiness right, present it right, and get the right results cannot be looked upon blandly or timidly.

The growth and culture of a babe in Christ is primarily the responsibility of the immediate church, of which the pastor is the key spiritual custodian. In its program and practice it is unmistakable that the pastor is the thermostat; his vision, planning, and actual routine touches and alters all things, especially at the hub and heart first, and in due course in the smallest detail.

B. Holiness the Main Line

Let us put to rest conjectural ideas about how much holiness should be preached, or whether it can be taught more productively in classes. Holiness is the essential line, the central thrust. Nothing, therefore, can replace it, nor should new, streamlined exercises switch it off the "hot rails" onto the sidetracks to gather rust.

Unfortunately, some may adopt the view that holiness is too complicated for "outsiders" to understand, so they suggest that it should be offered in a class and not preached from the public pulpit. Still others might say we must not offend visitors to the church who are likely to assume that we have a "holier than thou" attitude. Then, it could be argued that since holiness is a second work of grace, it should not be introduced at first, but at a later time when the presently unattuned listeners are ready for it.

Whatever merit these "breaking of precedent" recommendations may have, they are tragically braced with error. Though painless and innocent sounding, they are the initial steps to a fundamental breakdown, almost without exception. Those who introduce novel departures from the former way guilelessly believe that they are being creative and progressive. In good grace and wise candor no one would lift a hand against creativity and progressiveness. But such "new ways" are not in the long run progressive, nor are they actually new. That Isaiah in his day urged "precept upon precept" as a vigilant counter to idolatry and apostasy attests in our day the enduring worth of the prophet's counsel; its time span brooks well its justification.

What credence, therefore, these new measures may seem to hold at first, history contradicts. The record of history reveals that any degree of force or credibility lost to holiness in the pulpit has never been recaptured in the pulpit, the pew, or the assembly. Change and progress are not automatic relatives; change can go down as loss. A great difference obtains in the way Paul got the Ephesians and Corinthians to God and how the Methodists used the mourner's bench. Yet the important thing, transforming power, was definitely not lost. That method must submit to change is one thing, but to alter the intended original power and effect is another and a fatal departure.

Clergymen friends, let us all take warning. Holiness must permeate, fill, and endow everything a holiness pastor is and does; his preaching and his life. He cannot relegate it, or any part of it, to subordinates or other staff persons. He holds it as a primary state from God, and it will temper and slant all he is, says, and does.

The pastor's responsibility is enormous, but it can be a magnificent trust, a charge and duty from which there can be no promotion. Someone has asserted that there is no promotion from the pastorate. To be elevated by the church in administrational sequences is, of course, an honor and no doubt a recognition of worth. Lest we forget, however, nothing can or will supercede the shepherd's yearning love and concern for souls; his place is rankless; he is not in the running, for he has already arrived.

C. Precept upon Precept; Line upon Line

The caption from the verse, "precept upon precept; line upon line" can be taken too literally. For instance, to see it in the form of a rote fixed code, which prescribes highly detailed memory work, would be a throwback to Old Testament rules and regulations. This is precisely what holiness in the New Testament replaces. Consequently, we are not trying to substitute a new system merely, but instead love for law; a lineup of standards cannot replace a daily walk with Christ in perfect love.

Preaching holiness and preaching about holiness are

two widely different exercises. An enthusiast may preach about holiness without engaging the dynamic and reality of Bible holiness. This fault is not as bad perhaps as preaching against holiness, yet in the long haul it is not much better, either. On the contrary, holiness must be implemented in a clear-cut, well-defined manner to insure time and the proper setting for maximum reflection and grasp by those who listen. We must put holiness out where believers can relate to it, not "put it over" so we immortalize a doctrine. One prime consideration must be given: The preaching of holiness by any odds must be clear and certain as to content and condition.

In that vein, "Precept upon precept; line upon line" guarantees order and is conducive to clarity and understanding. For instance, holiness needs to be explained as to extent and content to unfamiliar believers. What actually takes place? Cast away the heavy-termed theological definitions, unless they are broken up into bite-size morsels for beginners. Make it plain: What is holiness? Why do we need to be entirely sanctified? What about carnality? What of humanity? Probe into perfection, entire sanctification, and sin after justification. Throw Bible light in these dark areas, for the most annoying, besetting questions crop up right there.

Once the groundwork is prayerfully laid, good things can be expected. This does not, however, intimate that the holiness quest must await a long period of training. Learning, seeking, and service can be in full operation from the start. The believer does not grit his teeth and hold on for dear life while he seeks holiness. His entrance into the Kingdom ushered him into a growing, active existence, with holiness begun in the moment of the new birth. Mindful of never-failing exposure to error and counterfeit, the pastor and church with wise foresight take great care to direct the way of the believer as full salvation beckons him on and thrills his heart. It is this sector of Christian experience with which the pastor, especially, becomes concerned and occupied, and so he preaches accordingly.

D. Getting the Holiness Message Known

Direct emphasis must fall upon the subject and doctrine of holiness if understanding is to take place and increase. Somewhat dubious about the perfection of any method, the author refrains from offering the "one way" to preach holiness, nor does he pretend to know it. After 45 years in the ministry, during which time thousands have been happy finders of the experience of entire sanctification, the author has learned that some methods work better than others. He has also become convinced that there is no single method that functions magically in all cases.

The believer must come to believe that holiness is the main line, and not an isolated adjunct which can be placed on the shelf when convenient. God is holy, Christ is holy, the Holy Spirit is holy, the saint is holy; it is holiness all the way. The author of the Hebrews rates it first: "Pursue peace with all men, and the sanctification without which no one will see the Lord" (Heb. 12:14, NASB). Holiness preaching, then, is not gathering up the isolated fragments of the Christian religion to form a doctrine, but it is rather the clear, unmistakable proclamation of that central Truth on which the Word itself and the plan of redemption rest.

Part of the grand design is to get the holiness message known, to get it out so that it can confront people. Not only do believers need to hear the message; they need to be captivated and charmed by its tender entreaty, to understand the extent and fullness of its cleansing grace. Then, too, the unconverted need to hear the summons to a holy life where the ethical triumphs over the permissive and right overthrows wrong. If we cannot offer the world freedom from the power of sin and evil, we undermine and weaken our appeal as well as our cause; psychological therapy can then challenge our best and match it.

How can a human being be holy? What seems like inherent contradiction must be ferreted out and dismissed. Often, deeply sincere but misinformed believers stumble over the problem of how a human being can be perfect. Look around you, my dear reader. How many convincing cases of perfection can you report? With trembling fear we anticipate more likely to hear about our imperfections, and often we do. Christians may misjudge and be mistaken; there is no appeal from mortal weakness and its well-distributed shortcomings. Only as the believer, and others, can reconcile perfect love with something less than flawless behavior can we grasp the true meaning of perfection.

Dr. Auer, in a Harvard Divinity School classroom, asked the writer, "You are a perfectionist, then?" The question of church relations had just been discussed. The writer replied, "It depends on what you mean by perfection." Because of his theological stance the professor overtly rejected Wesleyan perfection. The writer believed he knew pretty well what Auer had in mind; on that account he was not going to confess blindly to his definition of perfection. A valuable lesson was learned that afternoon in that brief exchange: Be very sure you understand precisely what your inquiring opponent means by his definition before you answer yes. How can a human being be holy? Read Matthew's account of the Sermon on the Mount where Jesus cited holy conduct for His disciples: "Be perfect, therefore, as your heavenly Father is perfect" (5:48, NIV). The character of perfection is implied in Mark's Gospel (12:30): "And thou shalt love the Lord thy God with all thy heart, and with all thy soul, and with all thy mind, and with all thy strength." As in Matthew the character of perfection is love.

E. Holiness as a Learning Experience

A major emphasis of the pulpit preaching should fall on holiness if the vast, comprehensive truth of the experience is to be communicated. Let it not be said by believers, "Yes, we've heard about holiness." Contrarily, it should be kept before them as a Bible requirement and a pattern for life. Every phase of holiness should come under scrutiny in an overreaching perception. The nature of sin, original sin, the old man, humanity, divinity, baptism, cleansing, second blessing, and the witness of the Holy Spirit all call for focal treatment.

If the approach goes well, the believer will gain understanding of holiness and hunger for it. The newly sanctified will grow in grace and the nurture of the Lord. Established saints will rejoice and revel in the holy climate created by the enlightened and joyful progress.

Artful in its beauty, dynamic in its power, holiness is nonetheless regulated according to a divine order, which gives it true reality for understanding and teachability. On that account an uncluttered, disciplined proclamation of holiness is readily conducive to the actual experience itself and to the growth which lies beyond. Hence, the principles and practices of holiness should be recognizably laid down, "letter by letter, line by line, lesson by lesson" if needs be. Whatever preaching method may be employed, simplicity and thoroughness are the goal.

Another point no doubt worth mentioning: Entire sanctification is a highly individualized personal experience. Yet one should never gauge its reality by the attendant emotions and thus discredit or impugn its bona fide actuality. Levels of emotional vigor move up and down, but the fact of sanctification is an achievement of faith in the realms of grace and knowledge. Quite obviously, as order and vital sequence take over, disorder and other ailments come to light and disappear, clearing the field for action.

The young pastor may ask for some arrangement or plan in presenting the biblical doctrine of entire sanctification, a preaching order that properly features and accents the main elements of the teaching. So far as the author knows, there is no all-embracing technique or way of handling the situation. Universal sanction is not given to any one method. That there are many wise, successful pastors who have laid the foundation work for entire sanctification holds a great deal of promise, however, as we consider the problem. [1]

For example, a series of Sunday morning sermons provides plenty of range for a depth study of components which make up the experience. Some of the elements of entire sanctification begging for detailed study are the biblical origins and roots for every single claim and demand, backed strongly by evident unity and balance, so that it will not appear as a stacking of proof texts. The high ethical bearing of holiness needs to be brought to light and thoughtfully described in sharp, vivid detail. When the Sunday School superintendent told the visiting evangelist, "Don't put any money in that parking meter; I'll show you a trick," he was desperately less than ethical. His trick worked, the red violation warning disappeared, and then he gleefully remarked, "Well, that will last till we get through shopping." Yes, until we get through shopping and as long as his unethical conduct is up for review. Why do churchmen indulge in such shabby ethical behavior and plead ignorance? Could it be lack of pulpit vigilance?

The community value of holiness preaching needs to be highlighted and appreciated. A California chief of police told a small holiness church pastor, "Your preaching has just about cleaned out crime in the east end of town." The chief said that crime was rampant, especially in that end of the city, but the message and influence of the church had driven it out. "You have done a better job than my police force," the chief finally remarked. A strong, active holiness church will pour forth into its community a restraining influence and ethical beauty; its value is thereby justified and enhanced.

Of special worth are the family values which can be noted and asserted positively. Church loyalty is a major problem in any congregation; spiritual esteem and excellence suffer when loyalty falters. The lessons learned in steadfastness, dependability, and trustworthiness not only favor the life of the church, but they form a safe foundation for life itself. Church members, young and old, soon find these enduring values good and helpful beyond the church walls. Holiness as a way of life always pays its way in negotiable coin; kindness, gentleness, love, peace, and Christian hospitality are welcome in any community.

A series of messages could be directed to experience, another to doctrine, and one to growth. The length of any series may be determined by the need, understood or expressed. When has any shepherd directed a pulpit message to the children, or young people, on holiness? The adult-sized preachments and exhortations are too often looked upon as religious curios by the inexperienced teenager. Could not holiness messages at all levels prove interesting and helpful? Not to prolong the stress, an endearing message on holiness to the aged could soften or dispel their battle with insecurity. The holiness ministry can be so rich and productive that not a solitary person need be disregarded; no one need feel neglected.

F. The Bible as Source and Building Material

The average person who comes to God suffers from a mind darkened by sin and an imagination that is evil continually. For the Christian, however, broad and thrilling vistas of spiritual enlightenment open up as he explores the "high country."

Preaching is judged as good to the extent it speaks to these two spiritual wants: whether it "opens the eyes of the blind" and discovers fresh and encouraging outlook for God's children. If preaching is Spirit-directed and -anointed, it will convict the wayward in their sins, and at the same time it will confirm and complete the believer in the holiness way. This sounds like a big order, and indeed it is. In spite of the seeming paradox, the true Bible message on holiness will come to every heart within God's compassionate reach.

The one sure foundation is God's Word. Unless one's ministry is covered by the inspired warranty of its divine revelation, only the vistages of humanism remain. Fresh, fertile texts can be found all through the Bible; it teems with holiness. The idea is to get out of the rut and roam afar; the whole Bible is fair and exciting hunting ground. The refreshing call of the new, however, should not neglect the standard texts on holiness—changeless standbys which cannot be overused, landmarks of the holiness ministry from the beginning. The suggestion to search the Scriptures and not stop at the commonplace should entail the warning that texts are not to be chosen because of novel differences merely. Aim rather at core meaning to avoid shallowness, and let the true intent show through. Never sacrifice substance for a nitty-gritty surprise or a new wrinkle.

Depart from hackneyed cliches; say it differently. Leave out trite phrases and the commonplace bromides. Do not interpret this to mean, however, that the familiar common speech and everyday language of the people is to be abandoned. To some extent the informal speech used in the particular congregation sets in motion a medium of communication; whereas forced, unnatural talk blocks the lines.

Explore fully by invading many fields of thought. Look into fields of interest especially related to the listeners, for it is at that point that their attention is arrested. Interpret the old in the light of the contemporary so that you will be speaking the language of the "now" members of the audience. An attitude of disdain for the past is by no means a mark of intelligence or a sign of progress. Yet the illusion persists in far too many minds. Equally true, the recent is not faulty or inapt because of its chronological point in time. Good sense and fairly effective logic will put such wrongheadedness to rest.

Finally, the Bible should never be used as a book of games. Search it, probe deeply into it, feast on it, and preach it.

G. Pastoral Use of Homiletical Method

As to a particular homiletical method, for the pastor expositional preaching is by far the best. Beyond question, no other approach will enable the preacher to probe the depth in his message as will proper exposition. By it the speaker can throw Bible radiance directly on any situation with convincing force and meaning. It will sound more like the Bible itself speaking, if most of the resources are lifted immediately from the Word of God.

"Expository preaching," according to Haddon W. Robinson, able contemporary advocate, "is the communication of a biblical concept, derived from and transmitted through a historical, grammatical, and literary study of a passage in its context, which the Holy Spirit first applies to the personality and experience of the preacher, then through him to his hearers."[2]

Unfortunately, expositional preaching does not fit conveniently into the programs of a high percentage of pastors. With all valves screwed down and the steam whistling like mad, where in the program of most pastors today is there time for the study and detachment required for expositional preaching? Nay, a thousand times nay. Most gallant men of the cloth are already loaded beyond safe health limits trying to keep abreast of the tide of programs and demands. Too often, it is an all-out effort to get "everything" done before assembly or conference. Time for study and prayer? When?

Thus, with Sunday coming, the pastor gets up early or goes to bed late a few times in a hard-pressed effort to get alone with his true responsibility, to preach the Word. A poverty of time for preparation does not forecast a bumper harvest, yet the overprogrammed pastor gives his best, and the results are often amazing. With no time for profound expositional dredging, the pastor resorts to textual and topical outlines, something more convenient as he works against time.

At this point it seems well advised to discuss briefly the grading or rating of homiletical methods. Professionals and practitioners differ as to which technique provides the best sermon plan. God-fearing, highly successful clergymen have used one or more of the established methods at some time in their ministry. Great traditional preachers were marked by their expository skills and power. After the turn of the 20th century, speaking very broadly, a shift to the pragmatic and functional forms was noted. The options and flexibility which characterized the new century demanded rapid change better suited to novelty and improvisation. Expository preaching fell by the wayside from want of time and devotion in the mad rush of events and activities in the church program.

Now, long after the winds of time have blown hot and cold, a new interest in Bible exposition is stirring in the sphere of homiletics. Seminary professors show grave interest in the rising tide of concern across the world, and better days for expository preaching can be safely forecast. Specifically, the issue is raised here to alert pastors mainly to the new vision and further to encourage the use of exposition in the pulpit proclamation of holiness.

H. Be Explicit About Holiness

Preaching should open the windows and let the light in. It should lay bare the truth in God's Word for all to hear. Do not ramble, generalize, or apologize; come to the point. It is holiness we need. Holiness is implied in many Bible verses, illustrations, and parables, but it is the preacher's task to make it explicit.

If the pulpit heralds are not fully convinced, if they do not find plain landmarks of holiness in the Bible themselves, they will leave the hearers unsure, confused, and perhaps dubious about the whole teaching. The preacher should never give the impression that he is straining at the task of trying to make something look good in spite of apparent lacks. Rather than mumble, stumble, or stretch a point in a text, avoid it. Use what is explicit and clear, that which you understand, and that which stands out, about which no one can really be mistaken.

The pastor compares vitally to Ezekiel's station and standing as God's "watchman for the house of Israel." As God's messenger to the exiles who lived at Tel Aviv near the Kebar River, Ezekiel sat among them for seven days—overwhelmed. At the end of seven days the word of the Lord came to him, "Son of man, I have made you a watchman for the house of Israel" (3:17, NIV). By these favorable odds he filled a key position in the transmission of divine truth. Since then only places and people have changed; the assignment has in no wise altered. Though far removed from that day, still no expression fits the pulpit sentinel as unerringly and timely today as the ancient eloquent term, "watchman."

Regretfully, such a brief and undeveloped treatment of preaching holiness pastorally must terminate at this point. A full-orbed treatise cannot be given here; hence an effort has been made to achieve point advantage and purpose concern integral to the undertaking. Even though pastoral preaching of holiness unquestionably merits long-range study and wide exploration, it must share time and space with other burning, beneficial issues to round out the crucial task.

Isaiah's wise counsel for a "line upon line" procedure speaks to our need and order with positive force and significance.

Part II

CHARACTERIZATION
(Variation)

Preaching Holiness

AFFIRMATIVELY

So then, just as you received Christ Jesus as Lord, continue to live in him, rooted and built up in him, strengthened in the faith as you were taught, and overflowing with thankfulness.

See to it that no one takes you captive through hollow and deceptive philosophy, which depends on human tradition and the basic principles of this world rather than on Christ.

For in Christ all the fullness of the Deity lives in bodily form, and you have been given fullness in Christ, who is the head over every power and authority.

Col. 2:6-9, NIV

Strong, clear affirmations have marked the resolute march of the Church of Jesus Christ as it advanced through trial and triumph during 20 awesome centuries, making known the faith "once for all entrusted to the saints" (Jude 3, NIV) that Christ is Lord.

95

Proclaiming the Calvary consolation and Resurrection recovery, the bold warriors of the cross of Jesus Christ bore this message of hope forward into a world obscured and darkened by the virulent stroke of sin.

A dynamic, growing fellowship attested the power and strength of their confirming faith and walk. The champions of the Christian way, avowing with great courage the stamina and endurance of a steadfast trust in Jesus Christ as Savior and Lord, carried out the Master's dictum, "I am not come to destroy, but to fulfill" (Matt. 5:17).

The Christian Church did not originate in the pit of despondency where the phobia of fear and dread rests heavily on every brow. Contrariwise, the Christian cause began in a positive, confirming life cycle divinely implanted and reinforced by the free, redeeming grace of God. Its calling was to fulfill the plenary purpose of Christian redemption, not to lay a path of waste and havoc.

The bedrock foundation of historical Christendom has been the Golgotha summit Cross and beyond it the open tomb. The Calvary consolation brought release and reconciliation to sinful men through the death of the Savior. The Ephesian letter records for us Paul's inspired insight: "For He Himself is our peace, who made both groups into one, and broke down the barrier of the dividing wall, by abolishing in His flesh the enmity . . . that in Himself He might make the two into one new man, thus establishing peace, and might reconcile them both in one body to God through the cross" (2:14-16, NASB).

Resurrection recovery at the open tomb cried victoriously, "O death, where is your victory? O death, where is your sting?" (1 Cor. 15:55, NASB). The positive note of victory has rung vibrantly down the corridors of history since that hour. Always confident, perpetually affirmative, the Christian quest moved forward to its consummation in time.

Ever a living issue, the Christian quest is alive with assurance, expectancy, and aspiration. The holy elevation of Pauline faith, radiant throughout his Epistles, crests in his Philippian letter when he acclaims Christ as his goal: "I press on toward the goal for the prize of the upward call of God in Christ Jesus" (3:14, NASB). He carries them to the mountaintops of spiritual conquest and triumph; his affirmations lift their souls in blessed wonder. Paul summits in expectation, "And we proclaim Him, admonishing every man and teaching every man with all wisdom, that we may present every man complete in Christ" (Col. 1:28, NASB). What a vision; what a responsibility!

As Barclay indicates, Paul believed that God was calling men to holiness. He so informed the Thessalonians in his first letter: "For God did not call us to be impure, but to live a holy life" (4:7, NIV). "Holy" here *(hagios)* signifies being different. "To be holy is to be different; it is to have a different standard, a different peace and beauty from the stained, frustrated, defeated life of the world," Barclay explains. [1]

As already indicated, Paul turns our gaze away from the trifling minutiae to the abiding magnificence, scaling the heights in positive strides of faith and dauntless courage. The God-intoxicated apostle, born out of due season, speaks in direct, point-blank language to the holiness movement today. While it is true that he pursues the lofty elevation of optimism, it should be remembered that the negative comes under his rigorous, piercing condemnation in its turn. In the Roman Epistle Paul plumbs the negative depth: "For the wrath of God is revealed from heaven against all ungodliness and unrighteousness of men, who suppress the truth in unrighteousness" (1:18, NASB). The great apostle did not suffer from a weak, uneasy alternate, as some do; each in its place, the positive and negative, was exposed to the critical regard of his comprehensive mind. Misdirected zeal may fall on either alternative alone at the expense of wholeness and harmony.

To preach holiness, the full-orbed approach must be declared. Overemphasis on either the positive or the negative tends to cloud the insight and, eventually, divert the truth off course. They are not polar states, but more accurately complements of a single verity; either apart from the other means nothing especially and goes nowhere practically. Only when the true force of both is brought to bear on our thinking can we hope for thoroughness and completeness. Even then it is possible to examine each in its most effective use.

If we propose to engage the strength and enduring quality of a cause, the emphasis would naturally come to rest on the affirmative or positive. In this thesis, the author strives to ascertain and stress the potent and functional values in holiness. Hence, the investigation turns in the direction of the affirmative with its constructive forward look.

A. Holiness Is Positive, Purposive, Pervasive

1. The case for a **positive** holiness does not contend that it has no negative relations. Holiness demands that sin must go, and that involves negation. However, it should be understood that no amount of subtraction can bring about the positive state of being holy, or the actual life of holiness. Thus, holiness is more than the deprivation of evil, or a negative vacuum.

Holiness is more than the absence of evil; it is also the living presence of the holy "Other." To Peter's first letter's negative assessment, "Now that you have purified yourselves by obeying the truth" (1:22, NIV), Paul joins the strong positive, "Christ in you, the hope of glory" (Col. 1: 27, NASB).

Affirmation does not eliminate the need of negation.

Because we accept holiness as a positive reality, it should in no way reduce the importance of the vital work of negation which precedes it. As surely as holiness requires an actual state of godliness, it likewise infers a complete absence of sin. Anything contrary to the nature of the Holy must go, without exception. That being true, a well-rounded presentation of holiness must involve the negative, not as a substitute for but a complement of the positive. The failure to fix, determine, or identify with precision the bilateral relation of the positive and negative has left rifts and ruptures in the church body through much of its history.

2. **Purpose** must underlie the preaching of holiness. There is a sound, biblical reason for it, not only to separate the needy soul from sin unto salvation and oneness with God, but also to make certain that his confidence and security are in Christ. Calling us "conquerors through him who loved us," Paul sweeps away the last barrier in his Roman Epistle:

> For I am convinced that neither death nor life, neither angels nor demons, neither the present nor the future, nor any powers, neither height nor depth, nor anything else in all creation, will be able to separate us from the love of God that is in Christ Jesus our Lord.
> *(8:37-39, NIV)*

Holiness is not a luxury or a doctrinal embellishment; it is the only credential for fellowship with God, in time or eternity. Therefore, the purpose or design in preaching holiness is to gain a perspective or a universe of thought with the Holy as its sun. Christ thus becomes the Axis around which all else turns and takes its bearing.

3. Holiness is not only the pivot of preaching, it must fully **pervade** it. It must be diffused throughout every part and parcel of Bible preaching. Preaching may not bear directly on holiness; but if it is Christ-centered, it cannot bear separation from it either. Preaching that does not in

some degree involve holiness does not in any real sense include Christ.

B. Declaration, Confirmation, Testimony

1. Holiness is not a proposition to be debated, but a pronouncement to be **declared.** Therefore, it is not dialogue material, which can be subjected to the will, whims, and wisdom of men; nor is it a syllogism to be deduced; indeed, rather, it is a truth to be proclaimed.

The preacher who signals blandly that he will not preach it until he fully understands it inadvertently places himself in the same class as those who say they will not seek holiness until they "see through" it. The call to preach is a call to declare the whole counsel of God as the Bible reveals it. May understanding deepen and light come to darkened vision, but through it all let us not forget that the preacher's responsibility is to faithfully declare the Word of God.

Such an evaluation does not necessarily preclude intense study, the right to raise relevant questions, and a place for honest disagreement. Maturing persons seek to run down distinct and discrete opinions, and they should not be excluded from the "ripening fruit" classification of learners. But to cast the profound doctrine of entire sanctification into the midst of an enthusiastic, yet lettuce-green group of freshmen for dialogue in the college classroom, for instance, could be an oversight of immeasurable proportions. The writer had to face such an ordeal when someone proposed that our Division of Religion and Philosophy "beef up" the theology courses by turning them into rap sessions geared to freshmen.

Haste not, however, to the conclusion that the foregoing remarks presume to shut off deliberation, or that all answers come in neat, ready-made packages. Nothing could be more destructive of motivational learning and personal initiative. The means of dialoguing are possibly more productive of learning for some students than any other method of classroom involvement.

The classroom situation is alluded to, for it represents what can happen in the church circle. Alert church members who are eager for knowledge frequently raise questions regarding doctrine and proof. They are in no sense truth rejecters, nor do they actually border on doubt. For those who want to think as well as feel their religion, there is ample room for exploring and inquiry. The outgoing person has to think for himself; what he believes has to become a part of his own thought process.

When we say that the preaching of entire sanctification is a declaration of truth, not a debate, we have in mind that it is an act of God and is not, therefore, bound by human opinion or judgment. This position does not cut off examination, but it puts all human inspection in the proper light on the value scale. To encounter reasonable, honest doubt is not a sin unless it calls for a retrenchment in God's will and purpose. God's plan of redemption is not up for auction to the highest bidder; hence the preacher does not plead for it, justify it, or argue it—he declares it!

2. In proper order, holiness must also be **confirmed,** which implies the removal of all doubt by an authoritative statement or indisputable fact. Authority for entire sanctification is the Word of God, which is linked to life's testimony as an indisputable fact. In Paul's first Corinthian letter he notes the weight of testimony, for he determined "to know nothing among you except Jesus Christ, and Him crucified" (2:2, NASB). Though in weakness and fear and trembling, his preaching was "in demonstration of the Spirit and of power" (v. 4, NASB). He had explained the true basis of testimony, "that in everything you were enriched in Him, in all speech and all knowledge, even as the testimony concerning Christ was confirmed in you" (1:5-6, NASB).

Holiness must be particularized in the lives of those who profess it. No amount of theology and logic stockpiled as proof can replace simple life-style confirmation. Right or wrong, the eyes of that congregation are sweeping the landscape looking for confirming evidence. The confirmed life so often can make the convincing difference. A holy life cannot be easily, if ever, refuted. The preacher who declares it is a walking confirmation of its truth, with his life, his deeds, his dealings.

3. A clear, ringing **testimony** is by imponderable degrees a winning part of a preacher's preparation. A strong, confident witness is an impressive recommendation provided the life backs it up. A testimony is first-person evidence of experience. The best tribute to a belief is a convincing example. Holiness must refer to a life, to an actual existence; it finds no haven or asylum in abstraction alone. One sanctified person in a community, living, loving, and serving, is worth more than six nominal holiness churches.

C. There Is Tone and Temper in Preaching Holiness

To be sure, there is pronouncement and practice in preaching holiness, but there is also tone and temper.

The sanctified man or woman is known by a certain bearing and behavior as well as by the content of life; the dominating character or quality is more convincing in the long run. Behavior here signifies how the saints react rather than what they do. For instance, the style or manner of expression, appearance, and everything about the preacher counts, and it will either enhance or impair the cause for holiness and God.

1. **Concern** more than any other spiritual trait identifies the Christian with Christ. To be unconcerned in the midst of need is a public denial of Jesus Christ and His love. Not to

reflect true caring while posing as a representative of the Ultimate Concern himself fails all tests of spiritual integrity.

When the scribe asked Jesus which commandment was foremost, the Master's reply is a kingdom of God standard: "'The most important one,' answered Jesus, 'is this: "Hear, O Israel, the Lord our God, the Lord is one. Love the Lord your God with all your heart and with all your soul and with all your mind and with all your strength." The second is this: "Love your neighbor as yourself"'" (Mark 12:29-31, NIV). Jesus thus earmarked the love-of-neighbor commandment with high relative importance; if the first is obeyed, the second will follow. The true love of self and neighbor is an index to Christian values. Concern is Christ calling, pleading as He did over the City of David; it is the love of God within the Christian reaching out, inviting the wayward and lost back to God. Concern is an inner compulsion, the impassioned tone of the Christian spirit.

2. The majesty of the Christian spirit is in its **gravity.** The minister is grave, marked by a dignity that becomes his position as an ambassador of the Gethsemane Christ. Fun and humor have a well-defined limit; the redemption of the world is not the pastime of a jester going through the traces. There is a grandeur in the quality of being sober, especially if it is reflected by the eternal seriousness of the Divine in man. Interpreted as "the sanctification" in Heb. 12:14 (NASB), the stipulation is stark and unrelenting; without it no man shall see the Lord. It bequeaths a sober, subdued respect for what is involved.

Long-faced religion is not a sufficient stand-in for gravity. There is not a single Bible verse to support a grim, melancholy outlook on life. God's sanctuary is a place of soul-winning and worship, marked by sorrow for sins, then great joy in forgiveness. All is not gloom and travail, but blessed relief and rejoicing, as the Psalmist catches a glimpse of it: "Weeping may last for the night, but a shout of joy comes in the morning" (30:5, NASB). *Today's English Version* renders it in warm and human wording style: "Tears may flow in the night, but joy comes in the morning."

Gravity is the majesty and mood of the Eternal revealed in human clay; indeed, it is a point where magnitude and greatness shine through. "And he began to be sorrowful and very heavy" (Matt. 26:37), is the garden scene where the Savior of the World bore the weight of man's sins on His heart. There the acute, solemn concern of the living Lord was manifested in the prayer of agony. At no point in time does the regal dignity of Almighty God become more apparent than when a crisis of salvation obtains. It is the touch of that gravity which grips the preacher's heart as he hears again the sobering dictum that without holiness no one shall see the Lord.

Because of the sublime reality that God is love, Jesus lifted up His voice over Jerusalem in anguished gravity and prayed for that prodigal city. Listen to His prayer: "O Jerusalem, Jerusalem, which killest the prophets, and stonest them that are sent unto thee; how often would I have gathered thy children together, as a hen doth gather her brood under her wings, and ye would not!" (Luke 13:34). It is that gravity of which we write, a deep, moving sense of the eternal concern so evident in the Lord himself.

3. The concept of **burden** comes up for consideration in any context of real concern. Once a familiar expression, burden is rarely mentioned anymore. Why it has slipped out of mind and is, in fact, unfamiliar now to the rank and file of present-day holiness people could carry us far astray by speculation. Perhaps the extravagant silence says enough.

Let us rather rethink the term in the light of contemporary understanding. Can the fact of burden fit into our present-day, high-programmed church activity? Is there time for detachment and prayer so often associated with burden bearing? Operational costs may be higher now, but anything so spiritually vital must not be controlled by inflationary prices; eternal values must not be priced out of reach; no cost is too high to preserve them. With this observation, we can relate the essential meaning of burden to our busy, overcrowded modern life.

To see and feel the need of souls in jeopardy, if we are truly Christian, is to sense deeply the responsibility we bear in God's great redemption prospectus. A burden for souls is more than an emotional involvement or state of human sympathy, though these may be a part of the complex. Instead, a genuine burden is provoked by love and the precious worth of a soul. Ever present, it is as enduring as love, therefore, and draws its incentives from love. It will not only fathom the human heart, it will break it. Until the lost and dying break our hearts with sorrow, we have not caught the true vision that crushed the Master to the garden sod. No second-guessing about what makes up Christian concern; it is the love of God in anguished emotion pleading the sinner's case before the throne. The secret of success in the case is judged by the intensity of the plea and willingness to sacrifice for its cause. Love stands to sacrifice all; it is not how much we know but how much we care. God works through all types of persons regardless of moods and emotions, hence the timid saint can also be a heavy burden bearer.

To feel burden in the right sense is to measure the needs of time in the light of eternity. A genuine burden recognizes the extent of the catastrophic loss of a soul going down without God or hope. Thus, the praying saint is seeing with Christ's insights and weighing with God's value scales the worth of a human soul struggling in the plight unveiled in the Bible warning that without holiness no one shall see the Lord. This profound truth must grip the heart of the preacher of holiness as a prime provision. The writer has taken time for a more lengthy discussion of burden on account of its imperative need. It is his expressed concern that burden again be identified as an integral element of holiness preaching. History seems very clearly to reveal that what did not come through prayer alone did yield to prayer, fasting, and great concern or burden. God grant that among our precious ministers of the cross of Jesus that concern will increase and intensify until we will not hesitate or be ashamed to call it a burden.

4. Finally, the hush of eternity must overspread the preacher's spirit and pulpit bearing. A need of **solemnity** prevails. Solemnity is the awe of the Divine in its sublime quietness. Every life needs the hush of eternity breathed upon it; every Christian needs to see the Lord "sitting on a throne, lofty and exalted," as Isaiah did (6:1, NASB). If we had a greater measure of the Holy in our vision, we, no doubt, would suffer far less from temptation by the carnal and the worldly. A holy solemnity will transfix and transfigure the saint, relatively speaking, making him a citizen of another world. We no longer have the problem of Christians being so heavenly minded they are no earthly good; in contrast we face a grievous shortage of heavenly minded church members in this increasingly material-minded age. Not saints out of touch with this world, but those with spiritual insight and upreach to transcend it and penetrate another sphere—the eternal—are in boundless demand.

It is regretfully true that in the Christian movement there are some who merely intensify the spiritual advantages; they revel and delight in the spiritual interests of the church only, giving little, if any, time to the salvation efforts needed to win souls. By testimony and much religious ado they give the impression of being very heavenly minded. Yet when it comes to evangelism, getting others to God, their places in the ranks are vacant, so that in that area they are of no earthly use.

It may wound them grievously to have this written about them, but they weaken, if not undermine, the positive thrust of the church. They do not seem to realize that they are enjoying the blessings of salvation without sharing the concern and hardships which bring others to Christ. They have given their muscle and might to the cheering section rather than the battle line. Let us not forget that while the honor parades have their place in the total drama, somebody has to fight the war, to strive, to work and suffer, even unto death, as Paul referred to Epaphroditus: "Because he almost died for the work of Christ, risking his life to make up for the help you could not give me" (Phil. 2:30, NIV).

The negative stance against the world, for which such persons have great disdain, not only keeps them from the evil, but sadly it also tends to keep them from the good. Let it be understood emphatically that this is not the time to manifest softness toward the world; if anything, our lines and limits need constant inspection and adjustment. An enlightened evil world is exercising the advantages of a vast stockpile of knowledge and social equipment to deceive and double-cross a gullible, unwary race. A trained, scholarly misappropriation of the funds of knowledge further exaggerated by inexcusable moral blindness has turned the whole destiny of man away from God and decency. Every anchorage of human well-being—religion, family, marriage and sex, government and social justice—has been deceitfully shifted to shallow water, the mind depth of humanism. So complex has the lie become that not one point of being or interest has been overlooked; humanism's masquerade is conclusive and fully realized. God's saints must be made aware it is hardly the time or place to relax their vigil against the world; they need to check and check again its subtle dangers. A misplaced radicalism must not reduce Christians' radicalism to retreat; because a few have taken extreme stands on radicalism, believers should not leave the fray and give up the battle. Worldliness still remains as a crafty, deadly threat to the saint and the Church. The margin which separates the child of God from the world is his first line of defense in the clash for survival.

Separation from the world, however, does not imply isolation or withdrawal from the world. The true disciple of Christ is in the world but not "of" the world, as Jesus prayed, "For they are not of the world any more than I am of the world" (John 17:14, NIV). To be in the world but not of the world is a beautiful, discriminating effect of sanctification which marks the breaking point between God and the world for believers and the entirely sanctified. The believer is a stranger in the world (see NEB); that is, he is not a part of its vice and practice; nonetheless, his labors of love bring him into direct and critical contact with the world every day. If he is to win that world to Jesus Christ, he must be with it in wise and serviceable activity which can be translated into soul salvation for thousands of sinners he can reach. The message and method of soul-winning evoked by the dynamic of the Holy Spirit fare poorly in the cloistered seclusion of a monastery or abbey. The saint belongs out there on the world's market where eternal souls are ever at stake.

To catch the heavenly vision assures the giving of a positive emphasis to the preaching of holiness. Ascribing to the negative its complementary place and value, we must in the process move on to the positive line with full affirmation for growth and spiritual increase. The affirmative stance becomes the preaching of holiness, for in the forward-looking optimism of the positive incentive and action, holiness finds fulfillment.

6

Preaching Holiness

ATTRACTIVELY

In everything set them an example by doing
what is good. In your teaching show integrity,
seriousness and soundness of speech that cannot
be condemned . . .

(Titus 2:7-8, NIV).

Holiness draws like a fire and slays like a sword; holiness is
attractive; only human defects and imperfections render it
seemingly unpleasant or offensive.

Because of the deep human veneer with which it must
costume itself, one might wonder how holiness survived
the first century. Only an all-knowing, infinite God could
risk launching the plan of redemption through human
facility and faculties.

Admitlly there is much about humanity which is un-
attractive, but when holiness shines through the veil of
flesh, it captivates the hearts and minds of those brought
under its influence. Holiness is attractive. For that reason,
whatever is conducive to its fullest revelation is always of
prime importance. Holiness suffers its heaviest losses

through misrepresentation; in fact, a great Wesleyan theologian, Pope, charged that misrepresentation was the principal enemy of holiness.

The world needs to observe what holiness truly is in practical daily living, or as "neighbor love." The world is more impressed with what the Christian does than what he says, and its reaction is positive. Take, for instance, the response of the people to the ministry of Jesus: "And the multitudes were searching for Him, and came to Him" (Luke 4:42, NASB).

As we have already set forth, holiness draws like a fire and slays like a sword. How well the writer recalls such a fulfillment, brought to pass in his own farm community in eastern Michigan during the first quarter of the century. A Methodist Protestant church, once on fire with evangelism and overflowing with holy zeal, had failed to stoke its spiritual furnaces over a number of years. Eventually the blessed spiritual glow for which the church had been known was gone. Revivals were replaced by church activities, services fell off in attendance, and the prayer meeting brought only a few faithful souls out on Wednesday night.

A holiness pastor from a nearby town held prayer services with preaching in some homes in the church community which had been opened to him. To these refreshing services a few members from the aforementioned church went. Their hearts were hungry for the living Word; long since the wells of salvation had dried up in their own church. Among the "panting" few were a farmer and his wife, prominent, leading members of the M.P. church. In due course, they both were wonderfully sanctified. Their presence made the prayer meeting in their own church; people came not to hear the preacher but to hear Mrs. Card testify. What a story! Mr. Card had been seeking holiness in the hayloft, and his wife was seeking it in the bedroom. God answered gloriously, meeting the needs of their hearts, and they came to prayer meeting to tell about it. The light of perfect love beamed on their faces as they praised the Lord for victory. Sinners and backsliders listened in surprise and rapt silence. The only complaints we heard were from the church members who were badly outshone because of their own dead, lifeless testimonies, which was the sad state Jude describes: "uprooted—twice dead" (v. 12, NIV).

Preaching, therefore, should make holiness attractive. God is awesome and wonderful; in no sense is He ugly or repulsive. His presence may overwhelm with astonishment and the consequent fear, yet the majesty and glory of His being will attract, hold, and charm. Even though the Transfiguration was pervaded by fear—"they fell on their faces and were much afraid" (Matt. 17:6)—the three disciples (Peter, James, and John) were not repelled.

A. Holiness Is Inviting, Magnetic, Charming, to Be Desired

1. The preacher's **inviting** call to holiness should correspond to the tender entreaty of the Savior, "Come to me, all you who are weary and burdened, and I will give you rest" (Matt. 11:28, NIV). Too often the preacher may seem to demand or order rather than entreat. Whereas no option obtains and the stipulation is without retraction, the gracious spirit of the Master must suffuse the earnest plea. The austere demand of the law must not empty the heart and hand of love. A brusque, demanding presentation of holiness void of tender love and grace can turn sincere seekers away, or at least dry up their enthusiasm. In all, and through all, means of persuasion in dealing with the sinner or believer should glow the warm and loving invitation, "Come unto me."

2. There is an entrancing **magnetism** about the Divine. Perhaps in the Platonic mood we could describe it as "The

Pull of the Perfect." While it is true the ancient philosopher did not use that precise label, the allusion is strong in his explanation of how the imperfect eventually becomes perfect. The title was suggested to the author through a book written by a rabbi in which he accounted for all development and evolution of the species as a "pull" of some intangible potential power resident in all things. That pull is exerted by the Perfect, so his book took the title, *The Pull of the Perfect*. The author wrote a review of the book for the *Port Huron* (Mich.) *Times Herald*, on which he was a reporter, not knowing at the time that the title and content were educed from the dialogues of Plato. Could it be that the rabbi did not realize that Plato's rational exercise in the problem was a philosophical fiasco, according to Aristotle, his protégé? Fascinated by the title only, there is a useful suggestion in the pull of the perfect as seen in God's magnetic field; He draws all things to himself. Jesus declared, "And I, if I be lifted up from the earth, will draw all men to Myself" (John 12:32, NASB).

God in His true existence compounds an appealing invitation to the human race by His blessed superlatives. He is by common consent true, good, beautiful, perfect, and loving. Who would scorn or spurn such a desirable prize and prospect? It could be that the world does not see Jesus in those who profess His name; looking on human ways, the results are not very convincing.

God possesses an extraordinary power to attract. This we are calling magnetism. The very mention of God alerts the mind of man to nimble watchfulness. There is something about the awe and wonder of the "Other" that causes the human frame to tremble with disquietude and reverence. A large share of human beings regard God with detached, mystical head-wagging only, yet none escape the arrest of wonder that His mention evokes. A genuine paradox is present in the divine-human encounter in most instances, notably the Transfiguration night in the mountain; God repels and yet He draws, fear and adoration mingle.

Again, a total sense of unworthiness may overwhelm the seeker as it did the tax gatherer: "But the tax collector stood at a distance. He would not even look up to heaven, but beat his breast and said, 'God, have mercy on me, a sinner'" (Luke 18:13, NIV). The centurion likewise felt unfit to entertain Jesus under his roof, so asked Him merely to "say the word," and his servant would be healed (see Matt. 8:8, NASB, NIV). Confronted by the holiness and goodness of God, the questing soul experiences radical devaluation of his own worth.

Then, in proportion, the immensity of God all but blots out the individuality of the creature. In the presence of boundless infinitude what self-image an intelligent creature may possess wanes to the zero point, and he trembles on the compressed edge of nothingness. Heidegger experienced dread (angst) as the feeling of being on the verge of nothing, but his atheism precludes God from the process. It is difficult to believe that God in His measureless existence would respond to the faint call of frail man, a mere speck in the vast expanse of time and space. Even the thought of it is overwhelming; the mind is swallowed up in mystery.

Then, perhaps, the semidarkness of wrong teaching hangs thickly over some to hinder their seeking, though they be sincere and earnest. To them, God is a hard taskmaster, bent on exacting the last trace of obedience at any cost and under all circumstances. A mixed-up counselee told the writer that he pictured God as a club-in-hand parent-despot watching every move he made, just waiting for him to make a mistake so he could inflict judgment. His own father had been a stern disciplinarian, demanding that every letter of the law be kept without exception or reason. As a consequence, the son was tormented by guilt and haunted by a nagging fear that he would displease his

113

father. The son had to call him each night by bedtime to make his final report of the day, even though he was married.

The counselee's spiritual complex revolved around his interrelations with his ironhanded father. The poor victim's father-image had been transferred to God, and only after a good deal of probing did it come out. Never could he please his earthly father regardless of how carefully he obeyed him. Neither could he please his Heavenly Father, for he had imagined Him in the same harsh, severe mood as his earthly father operated. On the second trip to my office we ferreted out the hidden cause of his trouble. A year later the counselee wrote his appreciation, saying that he was "just fine" and back to work.

Grace opens up another world for the child of God, a world of love and understanding. To view God as a lawgiver and an enforcing officer merely sacrifices His goodness and loving concern. It seems to the writer that God's most effective weapon is His beauty and attractiveness. In this divine appointment a subtle, ravishing magnetism works its enhancing influence. It is in impact positive, yet in sociability it is appealing and transporting.

The "Pull of the Perfect" mainly refers to God's people, but its influence pervades all existence. He holds His people in His magnetic field, so that we can say we are in God's "orbit." It is a spiritual, organic bond alluded to in the scriptural reference of Christ as Head of the Church, "because we are members of His body" (Eph. 5:30, NASB).

However, there is also a "pull" of the Perfect exerted on all men; thus God is, so to speak, the great magnetic Pole. God holds the world and all existence together by His power or attraction, recorded biblically as "and upholds all things by the word of His power" (Heb. 1:3, NASB). One must not assume that the "pull" is resident in natural things alone, to explain their cause, else the whole enterprise slips helplessly into crass, cruel naturalism void of personality or purpose. In that case, all that is left is history's feeble, ineffectual effort to explain cause and account for apparent activity in nature. God immanently and transcendently controls the universe.

Dr. G. Frederick Owen, noted archaeologist and author, expresses in a few words the "reaching forth and yearning of the human spirit in the direction of its immortal birthright—a desire for that at-homeness in the moral and spiritual realm."[1] Dr. Owen enlarges on the idea thus: "Man's deep, secret yearning for the better life is grounded in his desire for at-homeness in this God-created universe. All around him he sees not only meaning, design, beauty, and useful arrangement, but a built-in moral order in which all men have responsibility."[2]

3. In the unrelenting conflict between holiness and evil there seems scarce room for **charm,** but it is there, nonetheless.

Anything which has a pleasing effect may be called charming, especially if it fascinates, allures, or delights. Even a reflection of the physical can be charming; as, "The elegance of the painting lent charm to the entire room." In dealing with charm, one is trying to capture a quality of mind which handles the lighter emotions, such as those which please, delight, enthrall, or make happy.

God's holiness is charming in that it puts man in a state of pleasure or happiness. There is charm about grace and goodness, a feeling of good intention and well-being. Man is not that depraved that he does not sense and yearn for the true, the good, the beautiful in the world. He discerns them in God's presence.

The holiness preacher should cultivate this charm with the hope of increasing it. By it he reveals a greater portion of God's sweetness, loveliness, and attractiveness in his own ministry and life. That charm is more than culture, education or personal magnetism; it is the exquisite enchantment of God shining through the partition of clay and in the human ways.

Crudeness, crossness, and crassness are potent enemies of holiness. Personality roughness, crude manners, careless habits, or a sharp, cutting spirit make poor advertising for holiness. Very often people are not rejecting God, as it appears, but His professed representatives whose acts, habits, and uncouth ways nullify God's charm and spoil the beauty of grace.

4. Holiness must be **desired**. Undesirable people usually render holiness undesirable in the same measure they themselves lack its winsomeness. Hence, it is not the truth of the gospel nor the beauty of holiness which is rejected because it is not desired, but rather the messenger who repels rather than attracts.

Christ must be lifted up if the charm and attraction of the gospel are to affect the world. "And as Moses lifted up the serpent in the wilderness, even so must the Son of Man be lifted up" (John 3:14, NASB). All that is appealing and all that is charming and to be desired inheres in Him.

B. Hunger-Thirst, Inspiration, Interest

Traits not often identified with holiness have, nevertheless, shared its rich history. Some of them which are often overlooked or forgotten marked holiness in its best recorded days. The loss of terms need not be of tragic consequence, that is true; but if at the same time we detect a privation of substance, we need to stop and check thoroughly our maps and other travel information.

1. To **hunger** or **thirst** signifies a deep longing for food or drink. In the Word of God hunger and thirst are used to point out spiritual want and poverty. When a seeker cries out in his spiritual indigence and need, he is said to be hungering and thirsting. Few there be who have not felt the

pangs of physical hunger and thirst and longed for food and water. Jesus used this physical craving in a spiritual context to teach a powerful truth when He said in the Sermon on the Mount, "Blessed are those who hunger and thirst for righteousness, for they shall be satisfied" (Matt. 5:6, NASB). In Psalms the "hart panteth after the water brooks" (42:1). These scriptures depict the craving for God the human soul can experience, and seem to mark it as a prime factor in reaching God when the quest is under way.

The author believes that hungering and thirsting are indispensable provisions readying the seeker for entire sanctification. If an inquirer should raise the question, "What do you think is the primary preparation in seeking entire sanctification?" the author would answer without hesitancy, "A hunger and thirst for righteousness." Well does he remember the burning, desert experience when his own heart craved the fullness of Christ, with long nights of yearning and panting for the brooks of full salvation. Aspiring to perfect love, the quest for holiness became an all-encompassing desire with him, more like an obsession with neurotic tendencies ruled out.

The best qualification a candidate for holiness can have, therefore, is an insatiable hunger and thirst for righteousness. Holiness satisfies the soul through and through, as Paul gratefully tells the Thessalonians in his first letter to them, "May God himself, the God of peace, sanctify you through and through" (5:23, NIV). The need in the human soul for entire sanctification is urgently expressed in an insatiate longing movingly associated with hunger and thirst.

The hungering and thirsting of which we speak cannot be satisfied until the sabbath rest of the soul brings sweet release from the sovereignty of self and reunion with God is complete. That need cannot be superficially imposed, nor can it be experienced in a summary fashion. The need arises in the deep recesses of the soul; it is not emotionally induced. No wonder D. L. Moody stated, "I thought I would have died if I had not got it." If we are concerned with the problem of dethroning self and enthroning Christ, it is well to remember that nothing else better than a harassing hunger and burning thirst can bring about the death of self. The dying self is the price of total surrender; the czardom of the wilful self must end. No other agreement is within the divine forethought and provident care. It is at this point in the quest that many turn back—the price is too high. We do not seek holiness primarily because we see through it or understand it, but because we need it.

2. The power and uplift of **inspirational** delivery give life and wings to the preaching of holiness, elevating the best efforts to better heights, with new vistas of encouragement and enjoyment. Many of the old-time holiness preachers were known for their inspirational high places where they brought heaven and earth together in joyful worship and praise.

Rev. Bill Sullivan, director of the Division of Church Growth in the Church of the Nazarene, put it well: "Preaching that is an experience in the life of the proclaimer, lifting him above oratory and making him radiant with the reality of his message, is bound to give divine authentication to the pastor among his people. The foundation for authority in leading a church is effective preaching."[3]

Reports of radical preaching in the early days of the holiness movement need to be put in balance with the able, biblical, inspirational preaching, if the present-day reader is to get a true account. A type of evangelism based on fear technique and emotional manipulation emerged in various sections of the holiness movement, but it did not dominate the scene. Overreaching was the powerful preaching on victorious living infused with a motivation to be right and grow tall and useful. A high-minded plateau of heart-warming holy culture stimulated and edified the saint. That is a more authentic picture of the origin of the new, vigorous holiness movement.

3. Holiness preaching is not a deadening recitation of doctrine and standards. It can be **interesting** and challenging. If the speaker can arrest the seeker's interest, the struggle is well in hand. A simon-pure consecration to God presupposes a deep and extended attention span on the part of the seeker. For that reason, to engage the seeker's interest immediately is an important element in starting the chain reaction which eventually leads to an unalloyed dedication of everything, including the self, to God. If life is sapped and inspiration and interest die, attention tends to wander afar. Hence, holiness should be set in interesting and absorbing contexts, well highlighted by illustrations.

If, therefore, the wandering thoughts which ply the audience are to be brought under control, so that the import of the speaker's message will not be lost, then personal interest must be engaged and held until the Holy Spirit has done His work. It is of prime importance that a speaker become familiar with the varied interests represented in his audience. They are the open doors to effective communication.

C. Why Deal with the Attractive in Holiness Preaching?

The serious, deliberate reader with a yen for the practical, on reaching these lines devoted to artistic tastes and the appreciation of beauty, may well ask, "Have we not gone too far into the garnished, gilded area of the ministry in the proclamation of holiness?" Or, one might suggest that we "avoid the metaphysical overdraft and take a more rugged, down-to-earth stance."

The writer has anticipated a degree of critical commentary on the issues raised in discussing "Preaching Holiness Attractively," and he welcomes it. A thoughtful examination of the problems ingested can be profitable for all concerned. Beyond reasonable question, an attempt is needed to appraise the metaphysical dimension of the clergyperson in relation to preaching holiness; if any minister faces up to the spiritual qualities inherent in Christian redemption, it is the person who proclaims the holiness message.

The holiness movement is not vending a "pie in the sky," happy-time religious philosophy merely to tickle and please, to be sure. Notwithstanding, there decidedly is an atmosphere of radiance and grandeur, a type of spiritual aura, which accompanies the anointed preaching of holiness. This thesis, then, asks, "What are the true features which coexist with holiness preaching and characterize it?" Certainly, when the heavenly disposition breaks in on the human scene, questions are sure to rise regarding beauty, excellence, and attractiveness; the contrasts and conflicts will force it.

Whereas the stronger emphasis has fallen on the qualities of persons, which engage the abstract, it is sincerely hoped that in all fairness what is said in this chapter will balance out with a down-to-earth ministry giving symmetry to the whole. There are place and good reason to promote the aesthetic values and advantages in relation to the pulpit in every Christian church. Begin with the virgin concept that God is the ultimate Source of beauty, and the serenity of the idea unfolds like the waiting bloom greets the dawn.

7

Preaching Holiness

ARDENTLY

"As for me, I baptize you in water for repentance, but He who is coming after me is mightier than I, and I am not even fit to remove His sandals; He Himself will baptize you with the Holy Spirit and fire."

Matt. 3:11, NASB

Holiness thrives when preachers thrill to it!

The preacher of holiness will glow with earnestness, feeling, and compassion.

When the Holy Spirit is the guiding light and Pentecostal flame, the essence of Divinity will suffuse and saturate the person and conduct of the herald. There can be no substitute for the fiery, burning spirit of the entirely sanctified pulpit advocate who releases the intense power of the Holy Spirit. Therefore, it seems proper to set forth that holiness will be preached ardently.

In that light, let us examine what is involved. *Ardent* relates synonymously to many familiar words having the same meaning. *Synonym* is derived from the Greek, *syn* (with) plus *onyma* (name), literally "by name," that is same-meaning. Aristotle coined the term and defined synonyms as "words having different forms but the same sense."[1] Synonyms serve to enrich a term by extending its scope and value.

Among the helpful synonyms that clarify and reinforce *ardent*, perhaps the most trustworthy is *impassioned*, for it engages vitally the love of God. *Compassion* is love reacting to need. Included, with a variant of meaning, are such words as *fiery*, *zealous*, *fervid*, and *intense*. The point begging for understanding here is that whatever else may characterize the preaching of holiness, fire and light, with loving warmth, are the central factors. Consequently, this chapter will try to show the valid place of *ardent* in effective preaching of holiness, the author's best effort to show why and how.

A. Why Cite Fire as a Prime Referent?

Three reasons give rise to a special consideration of fire: first, its biblical import, it is stated without apology or excuse; second, its nature and divergent meaning which provoke different opinions and dispute; and, third, are we to regard it as a first-century phenomenon exclusively, or is it God's way of equipping and furnishing His servant?

1. Firmly and directly the **Scriptures** specify fire as an integral part of the baptism of the Holy Spirit: "He Himself will baptize you with the Holy Spirit and fire" (Matt. 3:11, NASB; see Mark 1:8; Luke 3:16; John 1:33). The baptism is not to be with the Holy Spirit alone, but with the Holy Spirit and fire. The reference to fire endows it with particular significance; it gives precise and peculiar pertinence to the Holy Spirit and His baptism: no fire, then no baptism either. Beyond a doubt fire always accompanies the baptism with the Holy Spirit; our task is not to say whether, therefore, but to ascertain, if possible, why and how.

2. Fire as used in our text is not capable of immediate understanding without explanation; its **meaning** is not obvious. Any attempt to make it clear reaches beyond the bounds of all material stuff into the abstract. There is, unfortunately, no analogous material thing or substance to which we can point to give it relative identity. One thing is sure, we are not talking about any type of fire familiar to us apart from God himself as a consuming fire.

Fire, according to Webster, is a phenomenon of combustion manifested in light, flame, and heat. Decidedly, the Scripture is not suggesting that type of fire. Likewise, when the fire of hell is mentioned—"But whosoever shall say, Thou fool, shall be in danger of hell fire" (Matt. 5:22)—no parallel is drawn to the fire in the furnace, regardless of the combustible substance used, whether oil, gas, or wood. Ostensibly fire can, and does, take different forms and produces different results. Nonetheless there seem to be interrelating factors which tie them all together, though manifest difference exists. Quite positively we can say that the fire in God's baptism, the substance in the flaming star, and the fire burning brightly in the fireplace are not of the same essential nature. Yet the characteristics of flame, light, and heat mark them in some real sense.

3. Numerous and various constituents made up the Christian **phenomena** in the first century. A vigorous issue at present among conservatives is whether the simple physical happenings which accompanied divine intervention—revelations and miracles—should be repeated in this century or ever again. For instance, at Pentecost there was positive eyewitness: "Suddenly a sound like the blowing of a violent wind came from heaven and filled the whole house where they were sitting. They saw what seemed to be tongues of fire that separated and came to rest on each of them" (Acts 2:2-3, NIV). Should we expect, therefore, in this century that the same, or similar, sense experience

will occur and attend every divine expression, such as the blowing wind and tongues of fire at each baptism in the Holy Spirit? Or, again, the "thunder and lightning flashes" at Mount Sinai when Moses stood in the awesome mountain to deliver the Ten Commandments; "there were thunder and lightning flashes and a thick cloud upon the mountain and a very loud trumpet sound, so that all the people who were in the camp trembled" (Exod. 19:16, NASB).

New dispensations were ushered in with a display of natural phenomena, and the purpose is quite obvious; it accompanies an important pronouncement. No reason exists, however, to repeat the sounds and sights, for the fixed intent of the demonstration has been adequately achieved. A small part of the Christian community today requires a rerun of the Pentecostal display, teaching that speaking in tongues is the sign of the baptism in the Holy Spirit. Because it is sense experience, heard or seen, it is supposed to add an unquestionable measure of security to the event. It is not without its perils and pitfalls, very evidently when the case is examined. It is either an absolute rule or no rule at all.

If any of God's people ever received the Holy Spirit and did not at the same time speak in tongues, the standard falls. The author is on record as one who did not speak with "unknown" or any other kind of tongues upon baptism, and he knows thousands whose testimonies match his own. However, that statement should not be interpreted to mean that the author does not believe in speaking in other languages; frankly and biblically, the objection is to making speaking in other languages a sign the Holy Spirit has come. "All do not speak with tongues, do they?" (1 Cor. 12:30, NASB). While the NASB is more explicit, there is no translation which offers any other conclusion. No, all do not speak in tongues.

A second position must not be overlooked; if anyone

ever spoke in tongues, or thought they did, and they did not have the Holy Spirit, the bold citation collapses. What about the Jonestown episode with its display of tongues and miracles? And that is not merely an isolated instance. The author is widely familiar with the history of the recent tongues movement, in which aberrations and abnormalities are not uncommon. An amusing example developed in our own city between the two factions of a Pentecostal church which had split and set up separate worshipping centers. They all spoke in tongues, yet each said the other was of the devil, without sensing the damage it did to the cause of tongues as a sign the Holy Spirit was come. If both sides were speaking in tongues (and they were), and both were of the devil (as they charged), it is pretty clear that something was of the devil; and it looks like the idea itself is the culprit. The only solid evidence: Tongues were not the sign; the philosophy of tongues as a sign categorically misses the mark.

Thankfully the blessed Holy Spirit supercedes the broken vessels of tricky, double-dealing signs. Jesus clearly pointed out to the disciples how they would know the Spirit of truth: "But you know him, for he lives with you and will be in you" (John 14:17, NIV). Here is a prayerful communion and knowing not based on the wagging tongue, which is a world of evil according to James: "The tongue also is a fire, a world of evil among the parts of the body. It corrupts the whole person, sets the whole course of his life on fire, and is itself set on fire by hell" (3:6, NIV). If trustworthiness had any importance, the tongue would be the last member of the body to be cited for such a stern and precise duty as announcing the unique and distinguishing Holy Spirit baptism!

Whereas clear inaugural signs featured the Mount Sinai and Pentecostal in-breaking events, overtaxed, routine labels need not be repeated every time the event occurs in the 20th century. How would we know if the "sign" is genuine? To resort to interpreters binds no wounds; all one need ask is, "Who will interpret the interpreters?" and the cause is off again and running. Only as a backdrop do the dispensational signs relate to the incidental cases, no matter how genuine. Except a sign can be established permanently, it cannot provide proof for sound judgment.

B. Why Relate Fire to Preaching Holiness?

A momentary run-in with the definitions of fire, which complicates greatly the hope of understanding what the scriptural distinction and import are, will not discourage our further probing and exploration of the vital subject. A review of definitions has served largely to make us aware that there are different types of fire, not one basic substance. Each type of fire takes care of an interrelated need in a total concept and system of existence. Whether these fires are basically one is not of primary interest now. We are concerned principally with how "He Himself will baptize you with the Holy Spirit and fire" relates to and affects the preaching of holiness.

Problems have arisen over the use of *fire*, perhaps because it has been associating with the wrong company. The loose, idiomatic use of the term *fire* in relation to preaching may well discourage its incorporation at all, or at least in a very limited sense. No effort will be exercised in this thesis to make capital of it, but its predominant place in the Scriptures warrants its studious, thoughtful deliberation; its lack would be a damaging omission.

Of particular attention is the fact that the Scripture order has it "baptize you with the Holy Spirit and fire," not, for instance, with "the Holy Spirit fire." Does fire, as it may seem to some, become merely an adjunct added to but not essentially a part of Holy Spirit? In that event one could have the Holy Spirit and not have the fire, if the case warranted it in God's judgment. However, if fire is one in essence with the Holy Spirit, no separation of fire from baptism is in any way feasible. The author stands for one in essence, not two substances joined in united action; "your God is a consuming fire" (Deut. 4:24, NASB). God does not precede the fire, He is that Fire.

In the Scriptures, one is struck by the prominent import given to fire. It holds a position and quality that cannot be downgraded or neglected without obvious intent; fire never appears as a secondary feature, which might suggest separation from its host. In that same sense fire becomes an essential part of the pulpit ministry; it is one with divine unction, for the Holy Spirit does not function apart from it. Hence, nothing is so flat and flavorless as the canons of holiness whispered, purred, or even shouted by a preacher whose heart is empty of grace and holy fire. Martin Luther knew of a popular preacher who admitted, "I always roar when I have nothing to say." Let us not forget, nothing can replace the light and warm glow of the Holy Spirit, not even roaring and loudness.

Paul's first letter to the Corinthians reminded them, "And my speech and my preaching was not with enticing words of man's wisdom, but in demonstration of the Spirit and of power" (2:4). The root word *demonstrate* here means "reveal" or "manifest," with the Holy Spirit, not the preacher, in charge. Paul is not putting his wise sanction on display or exhibition, carried out in human show or parade. Quite to the contrary, he is exalting the work and presence of the Holy Spirit.

The ardor spoken of here is more than human vigor and emotional reaction. Indispensably it is the dynamic unction of the Holy Spirit bathing and infusing the heart and mind of the herald as he reaches into a higher dimension, the realm of the supernatural. And we need to indicate it as supernatural, else we are bogged down in nature's haunts and habits. Amazing as they are, they cannot convey or carry the true import of what Paul is submitting and advocating.

The traits and qualities which accompany the movings of the Spirit of God, working through human vessels, are the same for all of his servants, though not the same in intensity. The Holy Spirit with wise, appraising insight adapts to the almost exhaustless variety He finds in human personality; hence, the wholesome, refreshing distinctions in preachers, of which we are aware. If disciplined pulpit manners render preachers little more than clique carbon copies, it is wrong; God searches out and uses the unalike, individual differences, making capital of the very personal peculiarities a homiletics professor might overlook. For that reason, the forthcoming discussion will forego any attempt to straitjacket preachers by reducing them to an authoritarian pulpit style often limited to a few academic categories.

Each personality comes already furnished with diversity that overwhelms the mind. The preacher as an individual human being need lose none of his priceless originality which sets him off from others. He should not, therefore, fall prey to those who would rob him of his distinct personal traits by allowing them to induct him into a textbook pattern of pulpit mannerisms. In this thesis, every effort will be made to preserve the unique, creative values and novel individualism of each preacher. Whether each of us bears a one-to-one lot with a mold that is broken on our arrival on planet Earth is a debatable question, somewhat inconclusive. Let that be as it may, there is well-grounded, convincing evidence in vogue that strongly substantiates the inimitable, one-of-a-kind distinction human personality bears.

John Dewey, the American philosopher, said that mind is made in the very act of experiencing. While by no means admitting all of Dewey's pragmatism, one recognizes that point that can be profitably taken. Every mind is a manifold of its experiences which are its peculiar own. No individual manifold can be repeated, fortunately; nor are all alike, else we would witness a plastic uniformity voiding all creativity. Imagination would become a prodigal to human intelligence, and the old mountaineer's poor attempt at giving directions to a passerby would hold. Unable to settle on a definite way to the place where his inquirer was going, he gave up in confusion and blurted out, "Well, Mister, you can't go there from here."

So regardless of how we hold that the original personality is constituted, one thing is inescapable: Soon after arrival on planet Earth, differences obtain; they may be slight but they are decisive. In that practical light no two persons can be considered point-by-point alike. What relief and what a stroke of independence and freedom! On that account, no one has to be a copy of the original; he *is* the original. Proper reference to one's own originality will halt any proneness to mimic or copy others; the best copy is usually only a parody, or even worse, a caricature. In following the example of another, emulate the good, but beware of mere imitation.

It is not the merit of valid imitation that is being questioned; the skills to imitate should be developed. Like all other skills, the know-how and proficiency used in the ability to imitate engage the imagination, man's most Godlike faculty. From this capacity comes inventiveness, creativity, and all ingenious talents. Therefore, keep its channels open; never clip its wings. Many a child has been accused of lying when his active imagination collided with the parents' standards for telling the truth. No moral guilt should be invoked in a child's dreamworld; it is the space-travel sanctuary for his imagination. He will use and develop it or be sentenced to a penguin existence like so many of his elders.

129

Therefore, it is not the values of imitation we oppose, but the tendency to give up true individuality, that which cannot be imitated and which wise people prize so highly. François-René de Chateaubriand cornered the right idea in saying, "An original writer is not one who imitates nobody, but one whom nobody can imitate."[2] The original writer may step aside for a worthwhile imitation and exercise thereby a true skill, but his genius resides in the fact that he is "one whom nobody can imitate." The writer believes that each of us has a precious vein of originality which should be traded off for absolutely nothing else.

We acknowledge readily the differences in person individuality, but as instruments of God in the proclamation of holiness precise correspondent traits are clearly evident, and the likeness is not accidental; they are Holy Spirit "breathed." As persons, preachers are different; but as preachers, however, they reveal a oneness and accord. Speaking to pulpit unity, let us now look in on some of the traits which relate to the scriptural provision "and with fire."

C. No Basic Conflict Between Holy Fire and Human Personality

The foregoing is set down to assure the reader that the author does not believe that enmity exists between divine fire and human intelligence. Enmity occurs only between God and man's sinful mind, "because the sinful mind is hostile to God. It does not submit to God's law, nor can it do so" (Rom. 8:7, NIV). To anything God himself has created He can prescribe immunity; but sin is counter-existing against Him and is thereby hostile and liable. For that reason, no hostility or state of war comes between God and His human creature until sin has gained the ascendancy in man's will, as in Adam's act of rebellion.

As the fire increases in His saints, God's presence increases likewise, and new light sweeps the psychological landscape, exposing many human shortcomings. Such an event would definitely follow an "infilling," which in plain words is a divine pickup for His child's lagging resources. In every case, the infilling not only brings replenishment of the supply on hand, which for some reason has subsided, but it adds to and enriches the reserve in store. The saint's imperfections and failure for want of knowledge are corrected in a deeply recessed learning process pointed out by the Psalmist, "The unfolding of Thy words gives light; it gives understanding to the simple" (119:130, NASB).

The opinion that any increase in the fire results in a corresponding loss in rationality and right thinking is palpably in error. Peter's post-Pentecostal homily is a prime example of how "Little is much when God is in it." His masterful discourse to the "men of Judea, and all you who live in Jerusalem" is a clear case of God taking an uninstructed fisherman and making of him an instructor par excellence. The very wells of wisdom were practically drained by his assimilated knowledge and effective execution; about 3,000 tasted the humility of repentance that day. The baptism with the Holy Spirit and fire augmented, rather than decreased, Peter's natural, personal endowment. For one thing, there was no animosity between Peter as Peter, the unlettered fisherman, and the imminent outpouring of the mighty Holy Spirit and fire.

D. A Vocabulary Approach to Fire Through Synonyms

John Ruskin recommended, "Be sure that you go to the author to get at his meaning, not to find yours."[3] When meaning calls for careful consideration, as it does in this thesis, the problem of facility is before us. What we shall use for resources and means to insure the best possible insight into the matter under study takes precedence over other concerns. To help carry out Ruskin's advice, every author strives for precision in word clarity, believing that words are keys to understanding. The writer believes that a vocabulary approach to fire through synonyms will light well the ramparts of agreement and clear thinking, thus making comprehension not burdensome.

However, any excursion into word study, though useful and exciting, brings apace T. S. Eliot's confession, "The intolerable wrestle with words and meanings."[4] The struggle is on and no stone can be left unturned; the reward may be in the least expected place. Perhaps one of the most gratifying outcomes of the "intolerable wrestle" is the way it opens up conduits of thought and enhances variety for more people, thus accommodating greater interest. To "work like a Trojan" would, in that event, be the author's labor and delight.

1. Holiness Must Be Declared by the Enthusiastic, the Fervent, the Compassionate, and the Fiery

As a minimum essential holiness is marked by warmth of feeling, the breath of heaven and eternity. The preacher of holiness must glow with it; his life and ministry must reflect the holy incandescence of God's love and lavishment. The true advocate is far more than a sentimentalist propagating a poverty program. He must exude an ardency typical of the white glow of God's holiness. Therefore, the principal attributes of preaching holiness fall in the following classifications:

a. A wholesome, Spirit-baptized *enthusiasm* attends the preaching of holiness. "Dry bones" apathy and lethargy will deplete the energy and work of entire sanctification. Zeal is contagious; enthusiasm is power. Lord Balfour said: "It is unfortunate, considering that enthusiasm moves the world, that so few enthusiasts can be trusted to speak the truth."[5]

A poor quality of human emotionalism may become mixed with any show of enthusiasm, it is true. It is equally true that without enthusiasm no degree of emotionalism will be revealed, not even the desirable measure. Apart from enthusiasm progress will lag, if not grind to a standstill. Another great reminds us that "nothing great was ever achieved without enthusiasm."[6] A cause driven on by enthusiasm can excite a crowd on occasion; whether that cause be right or wrong matters not at all.

Enthusiasm is a human quality which the Holy Spirit can engage and employ. It is a strong intensity of feeling, a spur to human intent and forces. It results from some moving inspiration, and then in turn it tends itself to inspire. Measured by any scale, a large degree of success in the ministry can be assessed to the honest, properly expressed enthusiasm of the preacher himself. It is an honorable way in which one's cause and interest can be extended.

b. Fervent means to "glow" in the sense of burning. Webster specifies that it is "very hot."[7]

In that special vein, *fervency* is marked by intense warmth and feeling in the minister's spirit, and it is used here as an equivalent of *impassioned.* The preacher of holiness, then, must glow with feeling and warmth, and the basis of that glow is fire. "He will baptize you with the Holy Spirit and with fire" (Luke 3:16, NIV). The cold ash heap from yesterday's fire glows no longer, nor does the idle fire poker by the burned-out hearth. But the Spirit-baptized preacher glows, if we are thinking of Christ's Spirit within; imprisoned Divinity—this is the glow, Christ shining out through the veil of flesh: "And His face shone like the sun, and His garments became as white as light" (Matt. 17:2, NASB). Again, "All who were sitting in the Sanhedrin looked intently at Stephen, and they saw that his face was like the face of an angel" (Acts 6:15, NIV).

A precaution is needed here: The radiance of Jesus and Stephen are not to be taken as physical, visible facts, which could transpire in selected instances, such as the Transfiguration or Stephen before the Jerusalem council, but they were not necessarily typical. The glow of the pulpit, for instance, is the recognized presence of the Holy Spirit, whose overtures speak to the spirits and souls of those who listen. All physical effects must be translated into spiritual equivalents.

Regretfully the useful and dynamic term *fervent* has fallen into bad company—those who equate fire with gymnastics or some kind of bodily exercise. On that account, many high-principled ministers tend to shy away from almost any staging or display of emotions. Even more regrettable, the cause of Christ suffers loss of the impetus and valid stimulation of a profound emotional drive. How then is the preacher going to deliver his message in the warm glow of spiritual fervency? How are the members of the church going to carry out the Bible dictum "See that ye love one another with a pure heart fervently" (1 Pet. 1:22)? Or, as Paul warns the Romans, "Not slothful in business; fervent in spirit; serving the Lord" (12:11)?

Fervent has been associated here with different assignments, else someone might get the mistaken idea that only a preacher experiences fervency. Fervency, as the Scriptures clearly indicate, is a quality of spirit. Thus, the human spirit has a passion of its own, a life drive that can be called fervent. However, the fervency of which we speak at this particular point is unique, in that it exists only when the Holy Spirit is present. The Holy Spirit's impetus does not replace the human drive, but augments and directs it.

c. Any attempt to define *compassion* may succeed only in emptying its great reservoirs of understanding without

134

much actual grasp coming to light. It is a full commitment of self-giving in the interest of another. Compassion does not hesitate to sacrifice all, even itself, if needs be. Webster defines *compassion* as "sympathetic consciousness of others' distress together with a desire to alleviate it."[8] Some hold that Bergson's definition of *sympathy*, "to enter into with," mentions the kind of thing which takes place in a compassionate moment.

To form a joint primacy for western democratic thought, W. T. Stace, in his book *The Destiny of Western Man*, proposed a union of Christian sympathy and Greek reason. As a rationalist, he quickly picked up Greek reason as the way-finder. But this found him lacking, if not void, in motivation or initiation. He turned to Christian love to move his concept along: Reason would find the way, and love, actually Bergsonian sympathy, would provide the dynamic. By that alignment, according to Stace, Western man would find his way to a full, satisfactory life.

Such a wide-ranging glimpse of sympathy gives some indication of how inclusive the idea is in social planning; it reaches beyond the bounds of religion. Hence, it is necessary to isolate the spiritual specific to establish the empathetic import of Christian sympathy. *Empathy* denotes the capacity to participate in another's feelings or ideas. Sympathy, in a similar way, is expressed in fellow feeling, an affinity, association, or relation between persons or things wherein whatever affects one similarly affects the other. The quality counts heavily in social reform, for without it the line of endeavor would be cut. When referred to as sympathy, the idea circulates freely in all group behavior. A naturalistic pitch would reduce the expression to herd instinct. But if we use sympathy to connote Christian love, we do not mean herd instinct merely, if at all.

Yet in Bergson's idea of sympathy, "to enter into with," the heart of compassion is exposed. Bergson's definition is restricted in the last analysis to humanism; but Christian love goes beyond the finite limits to the sublime. How, then, shall we define *compassion*? It is indeed the capacity to enter into with the feelings and interests of another, but it has a plus factor in the act of Christian love. It is human feeling and concern augmented and moved by divine love and caring. Hence, Christian sympathy, or compassion, is not bare human instinct relating to apparent herd needs. Rather, it broods over needs which count for time and for eternity, needs to which instinct is blind. Instinct will never cross the boundary of time.

Compassion was a gracious mark of Christ's ministry: "And seeing the multitudes, He felt compassion for them, because they were distressed and downcast like sheep without a shepherd" (Matt. 9:36, NASB). The Psalmist caught the vision: "But thou, O Lord, art a God full of compassion, and gracious, longsuffering, and plenteous in mercy and truth" (86:15). The followers of Jesus revealed that same compassion. In his reference to the Samaritan, Luke writes, "And when he saw him, he felt compassion" (10:33, NASB). Sympathy is at least a feeling for someone, and any human being may experience it; but Christian compassion is an ultimate concern, fresh and warm with God's redeeming love, expressed only by those who possess the Holy Spirit.

d. Fiery has its principal reference in John's announcement regarding Jesus, "He Himself will baptize you with the Holy Spirit and fire" (Matt. 3:11, NASB). Confusingly enough, all the fires we know anything about do not add up to God, which raises the suspicion that God is a kind of fire outside our acquaintance. When the writer of the Hebrews pointed out that "our God is a consuming fire" (12:29), what precisely did he mean?

A "willing to tackle anything" metaphysics class, taught by the writer at Eastern Nazarene College, explored the question of fire in the Scriptures and in the world with what facility was available. The objective was to determine, if possible, what parallels existed between God as fire and the hot heat of the hydrogen bomb. Dr. Robert Maybury, head of the Department of Physics at the time, expressed keen interest and so was invited to take part in the research and discussions which took four or five highly exciting class sessions. He lauded enthusiastically the "detour" in college metaphysics as provocative, if not a bit daring.

However, the gap remained as big as ever between the "consuming Fire" and a hydrogenic blast. Why? Because there were no coordinates for an actual comparison. For instance, one irksome question is "What ultimately is fire?" To add to the researcher's woes, we could ask further, "By what standard would we know that the consuming Fire and the atom blast were the same or different if perchance we could compare them?" The joy of thinking was reward enough for the metaphysics class, though unanswered questions remained unanswered. The unrestrained liberty of human imagination brought new worlds into view, worlds that members of that class theretofore did not know existed. The prize token of their appreciation was the awakening of greater interest in how God relates to His world; they are separate but not isolated. Further, a Bible concept of God is indispensable to the world as we know it. There is no excuse or way for it to exist at all without Him.

Thankfully we need not flounder in a rational or empirical quandary; the Bible signposts are clearly evident and adequately spaced for our travel and security. Webster defines a *signpost* as "a post (as at the fork of a road) with signs on it to direct travelers."[9] Every fork in the road on the Christian's journey is plainly marked by a signpost; there is no need to miss the way.

The idea of God as a consuming fire establishes some landmarks and signposts. A quote from *God, Man, and*

Salvation is especially crucial: "The symbol of fire forbids any thought of cold, sterile holiness." [10] Its further analysis points out that "as fire is a deeper cleansing agent than water, so the fire of Pentecost speaks of inner purification beyond the expiation of water baptism (cf. Isa. 6:6-7 with Acts 15:8-9). As 'a consuming fire' (Heb. 12:29) God in His awful holiness will either consume sin from the heart or consume the depraved soul in judgment." [11]

"The holy heart is a burning heart," the thought continues. As Samuel Chadwick is quoted, "Men ablaze are invincible. Hell trembles when men kindle. The stronghold of Satan is proof against everything but fire. The church is powerless without the flame of the Holy Ghost." [12]

Fire as the indispensable adjunct in holiness preaching is by these references established. Rearrange the rhetoric any way conceivable, but one hour of that experience in the pulpit, when God bathes His minister in holy fire, and the servant becomes invincible even though words fail him. Let us repeat, for we need it, "The symbol of fire forbids any thought of cold, sterile holiness."

"Preaching holiness ardently" is the author's sincere attempt to show why and how the foregoing is true, to endorse that theology, and to adapt it to the pulpit endeavor as a labor of love.

Preaching Holiness

AMIABLY

> But now abide faith, hope, love, these three; but
> the greatest of these is love.
>
> *1 Cor. 13:13, NASB*
>
> And beyond all these things put on love,
> which is the perfect bond of unity.
>
> *Col. 3:14, NASB*

A. Love Dominates Holiness

Love illuminates holiness like the huge beacons flood-
light the majestic tower; love and holiness are inseparable.

If any quality in the human spectrum is compatible
with holiness, it is love, the essential nature of which is the
charm and beauty of self-giving. God epitomized this grace
when He poured out His love on Calvary in the imperative
rescue of a fallen race.

As the preacher in loving obedience and compassion
seeks to extend that perilous rescue to deposed, sinful man,
the essence and strength of Divinity will attend his efforts.
The quintessence of Divinity is holiness and love in their

purest and most personalized forms. Amiability is the reflection of those divine qualities in the life and ministry of the entirely sanctified pulpiteer.

Even though the term *amiable* was chosen in part to preserve alliteration in the chapter outline, a careful check from research, the author believes, will show that few words, if any, could provide better facility in this particular conquest of ideas. What can be asserted about *amiable* can in equal measure be applied to the other chapter titles in the thesis.

Familiarly, *amiable* is used to describe persons, whereas *amicable* refers to actions, gestures, or any bodily movement by the person. Inasmuch as this discussion will have to do with the minister as a pulpit person largely, it is believed that personality traits will reflect the author's meaning more explicitly and expressly. Hence, such synonyms as *agreeable, pleasant, kindly, affable, winsome, charming,* and *gracious* articulate the thematic intent. Let us preach holiness amiably.

Love will accent all pulpit behavior, and love by cognate consent is amiable. There is no effective argument against love: It quiets the babble of bickering and useless strife, lifting its pure hand above the battlefields of senseless and soulless momentum, prescribing peace. The powers of earth recoil helplessly in its presence; no need to presume its extinction, for crushed to earth it rises anew to persevere with its healing. One can in ignorance or anger reject it outright, but no rebuff or evil backlash can mar its face of unspeakable splendor. Love heals in the market, on the Damascus road, and in the throne room of the sovereign.

Now let us reflect on what all of this means when the preacher's life-style and pulpit manners are examined in relation to it.

The tenderness and compassion of love, the sweetness of temper, and the kindhearted, sympathetic friendship of the sanctified minister in fullest measure fashion a pulpit vessel fit for the Master's use. Such was Paul in Christ's estimate. Listen to Him as He responds to the fearful prayer of Ananias, who knew Paul only as Saul the destroyer: "Go, for he is a chosen instrument of Mine, to bear My name before the Gentiles and kings and the sons of Israel" (Acts 9:15, NASB). Thus pulpit culture for God is the prior measure of perfect love and Pauline dedication, not merely social skills and courtly manners. Paul plumbs the depth of it in his first Corinthian letter: "If I speak with the tongues of men and of angels, but do not have love, I have become a noisy gong or a clanging cymbal" (13:1, NASB).

The harsh tone; the caustic, biting word; the disagreeable attitude; and the bitter, acrimonious spirit are poor kin of holiness—in fact, they are no relation at all.

What a difference separates harshness and firmness! To lash and lacerate with vindictive diction, in a harsh tone and spirit, forfeits all claim to love and gentleness. On the contrary, a firm, resolute stand for truth and righteousness in a spirit of kindness and love enhances a minister's status among his people and in the community.

B. Holiness Is Not Spineless; Neither Is It Spiny

Holiness is not weak and equivocating; neither is it severe and abusive. Persons who preach holiness are not spineless invertebrates, lacking in strength and vitality. They can take a stand for right and decency, not fearing the scruples that challenge the grounds of conscience. Yet, that same bold, fearless stance is void of painful rancor or sharp, smarting despite. In short, it is not spiny.

You can catch more believers with love than you can with a lash! Preaching holiness amiably calls for several outstanding Christian qualities, all familiar to Bible lovers. Let us give thought to them.

1. Holiness Preaching Is Kind.

The Bible classic reads, "Charity suffereth long, and is kind" (1 Cor. 13:4).

In the Scriptures God is portrayed as kind: "For He Himself is kind to ungrateful and evil men" (Luke 6:35, NASB). Peter's second letter associates brotherly kindness with two of the highest virtues: "And in your godliness, [supply] brotherly kindness, and in your brotherly kindness, Christian love" (1:7, NASB). Paul admonishes the Ephesians: "And be kind to one another, tenderhearted, forgiving each other, just as God in Christ also has forgiven you" (4:32, NASB).

In these and many other scriptures we learn what true kindness is: It is love in action. It is being Godlike and therefore forgiving.

Kindness is marked by tenderheartedness. Perhaps we should decide what it means to be tenderhearted, for it can posit wrong ideas, probably according to the company it keeps. Sadly and mistakenly, some take it to mean soft or maudlin, and perhaps melodramatic, thus yielding obsessively to tear-jerking. How cruel the error and how crude the application!

A tenderhearted preacher is one who is easily moved to love, pity, or sorrow for others in distress. Its best equivalent, very likely, would be compassion. The kind are tenderhearted; they get the signal when others are in need. We are not alluding to a professional, or a rational, indulgence. Response to need is not a convenient pause for a bit of tolerance, feeling the impulse to pass by on the other side of the road, but too conscious of public opinion to do so. So-called bleeding hearts are as plentiful as the priest and Levite, but hearts that truly bleed in tender response to the call for help are as rare as the Good Samaritan. It is this rare quality of which Paul speaks to the Ephesians.

Then kindness is gentle, forbearing. How a dynamic, high-powered pastor can assimilate gentleness and be forceful, yet be serene and tender, is mystifying to many church members who gladly welcome it. Strange combinations work like magic when the Holy Spirit is in control, a mystery we need not fear. Large, two-fisted men can be tender and compassionate, hence gentle and understanding. It will spring gracefully from a pleasant spiritual nature. No mark is more genuinely Christian than kindness.

Ella Wheeler Wilcox, in *The World's Need*, reminds us, "So many gods, so many creeds, so many paths that wind and wind; / While just the art of being kind is all the sad world needs."

Julia Carney, in *Little Things*, gives her sanction: "Little deeds of kindness, little words of love, / Help to make earth happy, like the heaven above" (later reading of second line: "Make the earth an Eden").

2. Holiness Is Affable, or Pleasant and Agreeable.

Holiness is sociable, not withdrawn and unfriendly. Not only is holiness a good mixer, it has the good grace and form to carry out its mission: "The harvest is plentiful, but the laborers are few; therefore beseech the Lord of the harvest to send out laborers into His harvest. Go your ways; behold, I send you out as lambs in the midst of wolves" (Luke 10:2-3, NASB).

Regrettably some confuse separation from the world with isolation and on that account withdraw into monastic detachment from the world, only going into the world when the necessities of life demand it. Otherwise, they separate from the world in a sort of religious exile; the farther they can get away from the world, the holier they believe themselves to be. But in the teaching of the Bible, separation from the world does not command or entail isolation, as John's record of the Lord's high-priestly prayer reveals. The disciples are to be in the world but "not of the world, even as I am not of the world" (17:14). *In* the world but not *of* it is the essential requirement.

Separation from the world is not retreat, not abdication and surrender. Not by any means. The break with the world is spiritual and moral. That break must be abrupt and uncompromising; no one should be criticized for a total and final rejection of the worldly spirit and the worldly ways involved in not being *of* the world. Nor should so-called liberated Christian professors look upon those who settle for the "old-fashioned religion" as backward and old fogyish. Else we may be compelled to think again the true import of liberty. Separation from the world is needed, to be sure, but in no moral and useful sense should the saints be isolated. The war of redemption is on, and we must carry the fight to the enemy. Indeed, we are not to be isolated in cloistered shelters and closets, lighting candles and intoning pious prayer. We belong out there where the battle for souls is waged day and night; right out there in the enemy's territory, *in* the world.

Instead of a "holier than thou" attitude, holiness people carry out Paul's suggestions to the Romans, "Rejoice with those who rejoice, and weep with those who weep" (12:15, NASB). The gracious lady, the well-disposed gentleman are in line to observe Paul's further counsel, "practicing hospitality" (v. 13, NASB). In fact, the easily offended, thin-skinned rank and file of humankind, in the church or outside, could profit by the apostle's guidelines recorded in Romans 12, especially from verses 6-21. Here the social affability of the church is addressed, with friendship and neighborliness helpfully accented. Holy people use friendliness as an instrument of salvation; other people respond to true Christian friendship.

Holiness is not irritable, snappish, or grumbly. Some people may hold strict sanctified standards, but they also have a bad case of grouchiness. They are not holier than others, but they are pitifully discourteous and ill-mannered. They are not more spiritual, but they are more rude and thoughtless. As a young Christian, such well-intended but poorly executed holiness living provided for me the most dangerous stumbling blocks. How often the shock would throw me into a confusing spin, overcome only by a great deal of prayer and practiced patience. Time and experience gave me both understanding and grace to help me allow for the human defects.

Holiness is not a handicap in winning friends or reaching people. A holy life lived out in perfect love is friendly, pleasant, and winsome. It enhances social grace, it inspires good manners, and it steadfastly wins friends. The only handicaps would be the inherited or acquired feelings of inferiority, with other personal fears and inhibitions squeezed into a problem complex.

When holiness lies open to view, with a minimum of human flaws and defects clouding its beautiful horizons, it has an attractiveness through its pleasant charm and grace. The author is not assuming any farfetched notion that everybody will choose holiness and clamor for it; he has felt the cold shoulder of carnal hate and rejection too often to become a victim of such a delusion. However, he has also learned that where carnal enmity lies deep and indisposed, Christian kindness can crack the door of rejection for love's triumphant entrance later on. The Christian Church does not meet steel with steel, but in the words of Jesus, "But I say to you, love your enemies, and pray for those who persecute you" (Matt. 5:44, NASB).

3. Holiness Is Sweet-tempered.

Elevated by gentle good humor, holiness is congenial, not quarrelsome and bad-tempered. The humor spoken of here is not slapstick jocosity with its poor habit of jesting and low comedy; such buffoonery cancels out the merit true humor deserves. The comic, rib-tickling gags and wisecracks peddled throughout the social ranks have little resemblance to authentic humor. They are not really evil; they are not humor, either. Some have a joke for every occasion, and it passes as humor.

Humor is a quality of mind, typifying agility and discernment, giving mental activity a delicacy and finesse. Why mention good humor in relation to holiness? Because from its origin it is believed to influence a person's health and temperament, hence "good humor" and "bad humor." Holiness insures a certain degree of health, with sweet temperament. Holiness has its origin in health; humor is a mark of good health. An astute insight into alternatives, with a possible escape in view, is humor's most telling service. It is the line cut out for an agile, healthy mind and could not, therefore, be a run-of-the-mill product of jocularity. Holiness and good humor come together in their lofty, complementary association in human imagination. Joke telling may be developed into a pleasant expertise, but there still remains an essential difference between it and good humor; joke-telling is imposed on the occasion, whereas good humor arises incidentally within the episode. Good humor creates the value joke-telling tries to imitate.

Whereas the veteran churchman learns to accept human discrepancies and inconsistencies, the young convert may face them as stumbling blocks, finding it hard to resolve the confusing imperfections. A Christian is a saved human being, and sometimes the human clearly stands in blunt contradiction with an avowed profession of holiness and love. The question may arise, "How can a sanctified person be like that?" Perhaps we should admit that some things believers do are a bit bewildering; professors of entire sanctification are not the only observable offenders.

However, to profess holiness, hence perfection, in some minds greatly increases the size of the target.

Holiness is known for its winsome congeniality; it is not offish or socially belligerent. It is important to get along with people; either we settle for agreeable conversation or suffer the loss of communication. In a moment of disagreeable exchange a neighbor may get the first jolt of unfriendliness leading to eventual separation. Compromise? By no means, but well-suited compatibility and graciousness at all other cost; in the give-and-take, bear down heavily on take. In the ninth chapter of his first Corinthian letter Paul handles the most difficult problems in this social mix which exposes the raw edges of human difference. "I have become all things to all men so that by all possible means I might save some," he divulges (v. 22, NIV). Paul's holy candor and wise concessions work out gracefully as his plan unfolds:

> Though I am free and belong to no man, I make myself a slave to everyone, to win as many as possible. To the Jews I became like a Jew, to win the Jews. To those under the law I became like one under the law (though I myself am not under the law), so as to win those under the law. To those not having the law I became like one not having the law (though I am not free from God's law but am under Christ's law), so as to win those not having law. To the weak I became weak, to win the weak. I have become all things to all men so that by all possible means I might save some. I do all this for the sake of the gospel, that I may share in its blessings.
>
> *vv. 19-23, NIV*

Paul's biblically bona fide treatment of concession in its relation to compromise is history's best. He would surrender anything but Christ in the holy struggle for souls. As always, souls came first before Paul's personal preferences, pride, and power: "If what I eat causes my brother to fall into sin, I will never eat meat again, so that I will not

147

cause him to fall" (8:13, NIV). Unfortunately, deeply devout saints are often skeptical regarding any concession, fearing the worst, that it might be compromise. Since compromise is no doubt the most insidious entrapment for devoted Christians, compromise in no degree is acceptable. Nonetheless the spirit to give and take, to concede, when real spiritual values are not at stake, is an adjustment direly needed to get along with others who have a right to their opinion, too. We can do well to imitate Paul and thus avoid damaging compromise, yet devise effective and friendly concessions to hold our line intact. Mark it well, concession here has no degree of compromise, nor any suggestion that might lead to it.

Finally, holiness is pleasing to both sight and sound. The author is fully conscious that he is putting his head in the lion's mouth; but, on account of pressure, not for pleasure. Holiness is godliness abroad, or love at large. The sanctified person is its point of revelation. Whatever conduces to being the best representative of the blessed grace of entire sanctification is without question of prime importance. The secret: Give love unimpeded freedom! "Sir, we would see Jesus," or we wish to see Jesus (John 12:21). Had the Greeks who had gone up to the feast at Jerusalem encountered so many poor proxy substitutes for Jesus that they wanted to see for themselves the striking Figure of whom the Pharisees had lamented, "The world has gone after Him" (v. 19, NASB)? Or were they merely pursuing a normal social interest? Whatever the excuse the import is evident: They wanted unobstructed sight of Him. They wanted to see if what they had heard could be true of anyone.

Could it be that many people today approach the profession of holiness—perfection—in the same skeptical mood? They, like the Greeks, want to see for themselves. And they, as did the Greeks, have every right to inspect the goods Christianity advertises. The Greeks could have chosen no better example than the Master himself. That privilege and joy we cannot repeat by sight, but His holy way is obvious to those who will look honestly at His account in the Word of God. The saint of any age is a true pattern of the original Prototype, a standard and typical example of the Christ the Greeks asked Philip to see.

A sobering thought, indeed, is: What would the Greeks see if they came to our Jerusalem now to worship? Would they see the overflowing fountains of love we should be, or the picayune, niggling, poor examples we so often are? Our problem is not out-broken sin, not even a slightly bent intent, but the proneness to niggle, to spend too much effort on minor details or find fault constantly in a petty way. Paul's treatment of concession was a masterpiece on niggling saints.

How often, and how tragically, some have pushed and struggled for a particular music or worship posture in the church, while others concentrated on a picky dress detail only to bring stress and division into the body of Christ and eventually confusion into the community. Sankey's gospel music shocked conventional England; it was new, it was different. On the contrary it has become the conventional expression of the 20th century; hence it is not evil or wrong. True to trend, if a 20th-century saint stepped on a platform in Wesley's day in slacks or a below-the-knee dress, she would have been taken for an evil woman. Dresses that did not conceal the ankles at the turn of the century would arouse piddling comment in camp meeting circles, and especially in the church.

The author has sought to develop an appreciation for all music; he has not succeeded in every case. Music not to our personal taste is not wicked on that account. Fortunately there is a rather generous selection. Then to stereotype a worship service does not thereby mark its identity with godliness.

To travel extensively is a music and worship treat, to see how people all over the world have resolved these needs. Often it is ingenious, it is beautiful, but it is not American. As the writer sat in his room in south India, waiting for the service to begin, the "choir" and "orchestra" were warming up. They banged and rattled anything that would make a noise. The normal reaction to such a scene would no doubt be "What a clattering din!" Contrariwise the sounds filled the writer's soul with joy that has not diminished after a busy decade; for joy was the very essence of their expression. Even now the throb of that nondescript orchestra and choir stirs the writer's spirit, and the joy they conveyed fill his soul afresh. Clearly it is not the music or singing but what is in it that makes the difference to the saint; holy joy will bless his soul regardless of the transportation facilities.

Deeply sincere saints have become entangled in church troubles related to standards, only to lose their sweetness and spiritual warmth. They did not "hold the line," nor did they demonstrate their first love; they failed both. Whatever happens to standards and local customs is one thing; we must meet Peter's First Epistle exhortation to "love one another deeply, from the heart" (1:22, NIV). A sour profession of religion begets only roots of bitterness and division.

Yet from the foregoing let us not assume that standards and guidelines are passé or out. Far be it from us to think such ideas, for love as a pure, perfect measure is more exacting in its moral and ethical demands than man's rules of conduct at their rational best. Standards challenge the will, but love searches the heart.

It is worth repetition here: You can catch more people with love than you can with a lash!

4. Finally, Holiness Is Love in Action.

Inertia touched by love explodes into concerted action; docility and do-nothingness do not exist on friendly terms, but their ways soon part. If anything will release love in the community, entire sanctification with its prime motivation in perfect love will do it.

To love God with all the heart, soul, mind, and strength is a miracle of grace. No person can love perfectly apart from God's grace. Love can be perfect and still be immature; it can be complete and yet not fully developed or full-grown. When we talk about perfect love, we are identifying it as to kind; its character is undefiled. It can be pure in state and not mature in process. Pure love grows and develops as a perfect child fills out and grows up. He was a perfect baby when born, he was "all boy" as the process moved on, and he is "all man" now that he is grown, but all along the line from birth to maturity he was a perfect being. The young Christian is not mature, or full-grown, but that new saint can love God perfectly (Mark 12:30-31). His love is in kind, perfect, but his growth is in degree, imperfect.

A renowned theologian told the author that so long as a human being is involved in the above process, everything would have to be in degree, perfection being out of the question. No exception can be made even in man's full surrender or his all-out commitment. That too is in degree, largely because man is not absolute. On that account, existential autonomy cannot really be spoken of man, for the sliding scale of degree forbids that. How man can avoid being absorbed into the Absolute is far from clear. If a Christian cannot be tangibly all-out for God, autonomy is meaningless and guilt cannot be fixed. When all is said and done, the Scripture assumes that the saint's commitment is all-out and all-consuming, else why implicate *all* at all? The holy men who transcribed God's Word caught the intent behind the scene. Jesus did not hesitate to say "all" when He was speaking of how much the saint is to love God, nor did He drop the slightest hint that a degree situation obtained (Matt. 22:37; Mark 12:30; Luke 10:27). If "all" does not require 100 percent, where, pray, shall we stop when we hit the decline?

A maladroit slant on perfection, frequently used, should not pass without deeper inspection. How often have we heard it stated, "The only perfection I know anything about is that I am perfectly aware I'm not perfect." That's not bad religion if it does not stop there; or if the quest for perfection does not end in imperfection at long last. To be aware of one's imperfections is a benefit of God's grace, to be sure, but to bring the whole process to a jerking halt thereat is to sacrifice further growth in that same beautiful grace.

A damaging and painful dilemma protrudes as a real menace: If the speaker is jubilating over the discovery of imperfections merely, his religious safari is a loveless expedition; then, if love does not motivate his quest, he is without a true goal. To seem to gloat over one's imperfections is graceless and tactless; it should be a painful experience. Then, to stop there leads one to believe that love is absent altogether; for love, especially divine love, is a relentless incentive to push forward and upward in God's reassuring will. Thus, "to be perfectly aware that one is not perfect" can be a dead end leading nowhere or a decisive insight leading to victory.

Tender feeling is a comforting quality that characterizes the preacher of holiness. One could reliably speak concerning him, "The tenderness of his touch bathed and soothed the hurt." An atmosphere of kindness and healing follows him as he preaches or works. No matter why the pain, the loss, or the disappointment, the man of God meets each moment and contact in loving-kindness and earnest petition. He offers his services of love. In his preaching stance especially he reflects the favorable characteristics of holy love and total commitment.

Forgiveness is found in tender feelings and perhaps nowhere else. It was God's tender indulgence with a lost race that moved Him to the cruel Calvary crisis to redeem the sinner. That same tender affection prompts the thorough self-giving of the preacher of entire sanctification as he reaches out hands of love to his fellow creatures. In that extension of God's mercy the most saintly and beautiful grace appears, tenderheartedness.

Thus, love makes tender the heart, moves the feelings, and enhances the pulpit person as an amiable and winsome envoy of the cross of Jesus Christ.

The lofty peaks of love glisten in the light of heaven and eternity. Alert prayer and contemplation will further disclose God's love bathing the hills and valleys of life and time with pure, redeeming light. Preaching holiness amiably is the preacher's vital lifeline to that divine realm, which becomes his source and supply. He converges with it, and they become one in will, purpose, and character; yet because of freedom of choice he remains wholly free and personally separate.

The person who delivers the message of holiness has only one main restraint, the searching love of the Cross. Augustine caught something of the moment of the situation and spoke the words, "Love, and do what you will."[1] Paul Ramsey at Princeton approximated St. Augustine in his well-known apothegm, "Love, then do as you well please." Even though a great deal of needed theology is not within true focus, to be sure, a pervasive truth persists: Love is safe morally, motivationally, and enduringly as an indwelling guide.

In the end, let us see that love liberates completely. In His last hours alone with His disciples, Jesus spoke the words which put freedom in its true balance and perspective. He said, "If therefore the Son shall make you free, you shall be free indeed" (John 8:36, NASB). Thus, we are really free to do what we will; with this security, we will do only the will of the Father.

Strictly speaking, as sanctification is entire (complete), the love by which it is achieved is likewise perfect (complete). "Greater love has no one than this, that one lay down his life for his friends," the Lord Jesus told His distraught disciples in His closing discourse, which abounded with overflowing love (John 15:13, NASB).

> Were the whole realm of nature mine,
> That were a present far too small;
> Love so amazing, so divine
> Demands my soul, my life, my all.
>
> Isaac Watts

Reference Notes

Preface
1. W. T. Purkiser, Richard S. Taylor, and Willard H. Taylor, *God, Man, and Salvation* (Kansas City: Beacon Hill Press of Kansas City, 1977), p. 14.

Introduction
1. Timothy L. Smith, *Nazarenes and the Wesleyan Mission* (Kansas City: Beacon Hill Press of Kansas City, 1979), p. 7.

Part I: Certification
CHAPTER 1 PREACHING HOLINESS BIBLICALLY
1. *God, Man, and Salvation*, p. 462.
2. A clear-cut record of the biblical use and meaning of *holy* and *holiness* has been set down by Dr. J. Kenneth Grider in his recent book, *Entire Sanctification: The Distinctive Doctrine of Wesleyanism* (Kansas City: Beacon Hill Press of Kansas City, 1980), pp. 17-19.
3. *God, Man, and Salvation*, p. 34.
4. Ibid., pp. 34-35.
5. Ibid., pp. 466-67.
6. Donald S. Metz, *Studies in Biblical Holiness* (Kansas City: Beacon Hill Press of Kansas City, 1971), p. 52.
7. Gustaf Aulén, *The Faith of the Christian Church*, trans. Eric H. Wahlstrom (Philadelphia: Fortress Press, 1960), p. 132.
8. John Wick Bowman, *Prophetic Realism and the Gospel* (Philadelphia: Westminster Press, 1955), pp. 161-63.
9. *God, Man, and Salvation*, p. 179.
10. Olin A. Curtis, *The Christian Faith*, p. 15.
11. Paul Tillich, *Systematic Theology*, 3 vols. (Chicago: University of Chicago Press, 1951-63), 1:32.
12. *Dogmatics*

13. Church Growth Monograph

14. *God, Man, and Salvation,* p. 22.

15. *Italienische Reise*

16. Hans Jonas, *The Phenomenon of Life* (New York: Dell Publishing Co., n.d.), p. 213.

17. Ibid.

18. *Studies in Biblical Holiness,* p. 228.

19. William Hordern, *New Directions in Theology Today* (Philadelphia: Westminster Press, 1966), 1:28.

20. *Studies in Biblical Holiness,* p. 228.

21. F. F. Bruce, *The New Testament Documents* (Grand Rapids: Eerdmans, 1959), p. 71.

22. Ibid., pp. 7-8.

CHAPTER 2   PREACHING HOLINESS DOCTRINALLY

1. *Christianity Today,* April 18, 1980, p. 20.

2. *Nazarenes and the Wesleyan Mission,* p. 8.

3. T. E. Martin, "What Happened to Doctrinal Preaching?" *Preacher's Magazine,* Fall, 1978.

4. Richard S. Taylor, *Preaching Holiness Today* (Kansas City: Beacon Hill Press of Kansas City, 1968), p. 46.

5. Endymion, bk. 1, stanza 1.

6. William Barclay, *The Mind of St. Paul* (New York: Harper & Row, 1975), p. 48.

7. "An Essay on Criticism," line 525.

8. *Beacon Bible Commentary,* 10 vols. (Kansas City: Beacon Hill Press of Kansas City, 1968), 8:176.

9. *Webster's New Collegiate Dictionary,* 2nd ed., s.v. "belief."

10. Delbert Rose, *A Theology of Christian Experience* (Minneapolis: Bethany Fellowship, 1966), p. 207.

11. Charles Hodge, *Systematic Theology* (New York: Charles Scribner and Co., 1872), 1:54.

12. *Preaching Holiness Today,* pp. 45-46.

CHAPTER 3   PREACHING HOLINESS
EVANGELISTICALLY

1. Church Growth Monograph

2. Ibid.

3. *Mind of St. Paul,* pp. 42-43.

4. *Church Dogmatics* (vol. 3, pt. 3, pp. 255-56).

5. Chester Wilkins, *A Handbook for Personal Soul-Winning*, 5th ed. (Kansas City: Beacon Hill Press of Kansas City, 1972), Introduction.

6. Robert L. Cunningham, *Situationism and the New Morality* (New York: Appleton-Century-Crofts, 1970), p. 59.

7. Edith Hamilton, *Mythology* (New York: New American Library of World Literature, 1942), pp. 16-17.

8. For further reference and study on secondness one may turn to Prof. Richard Howard's recent work on *Tongues Speaking* (Norway, Me., Box 153: Western Maine Graphics Publications, 1980). Especially note the accounts of Cornelius (Acts 10) and Paul's visit to Ephesus (Acts 19). Both clear instances of a second work of grace in events, or crisis.

CHAPTER 4 PREACHING HOLINESS PASTORALLY

1. In *Preaching Holiness Today*, Richard Taylor has put together a useful orientation of advice, recommendations, and pointers worked into helpful homiletical adaptation for the pulpit.

2. Dr. Robinson takes the reader step by step through the process of preparing and preaching an expository sermon in *Biblical Preaching: The Development and Delivery of Expository Messages* (Grand Rapids: Baker Book House, 1980), p. 20.

Part II: Characterization

CHAPTER 5 PREACHING HOLINESS AFFIRMATIVELY

1. *Mind of St. Paul*, p. 50.

CHAPTER 6 PREACHING HOLINESS ATTRACTIVELY

1. G. Fredrick Owen, *Entering the Kingdom* (Kansas City: Beacon Hill Press of Kansas City, 1969), p. 8.

2. Ibid., p. 15.

3. *Preacher's Magazine*, June-August, 1980, p. 17.

CHAPTER 7 PREACHING HOLINESS ARDENTLY

1. *Rhetoric*

2. *Geni du Christianisme*

3. John Ruskin, *Sesame and Lilies*, Vol. 1, par. 13.

4. T. S. Eliot, "East Coker," pt. 2.

5. Letter to Mrs. Drew, 1918.

6. Ralph Waldo Emerson, "Circle" Essays.

7. *Webster's New Collegiate Dictionary*, 2nd ed., s.v. "fervent."

8. Ibid., s.v. "compassion."

9. Ibid., s.v. "signpost."

10. *God, Man, and Salvation*, p. 490.

11. Ibid.

12. Ibid.

CHAPTER 8   PREACHING HOLINESS AMIABLY

1. Augustine, *In Ioann*, 8.7.